A STEP-BY-STEP COURSE IN
OIL PAINTING

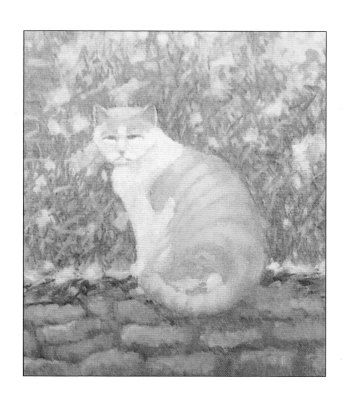

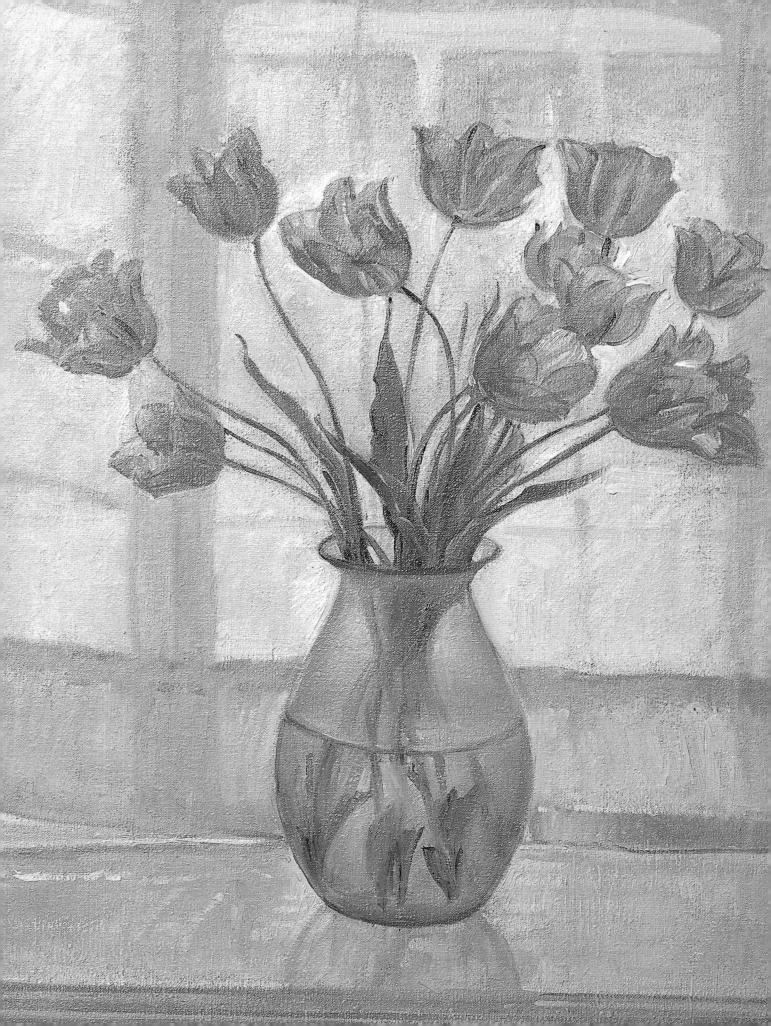

A STEP-BY-STEP COURSE IN
OIL PAINTING

A practical guide to techniques, with easy-to-follow projects using impasto,
toned grounds, blending and underpainting, shown in 185 photographs

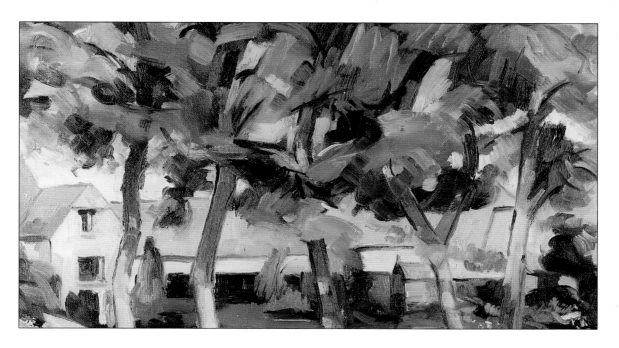

ANGELA GAIR

southwater

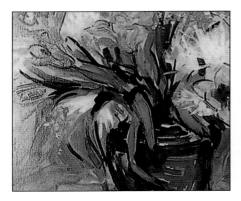
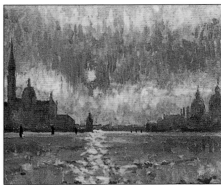
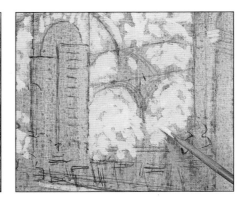

This edition is published by Southwater, an imprint of Anness Publishing Ltd
108 Great Russell Street, London WC1B 3NA; info@anness.com

www.southwaterbooks.com; www.annesspublishing.com

If you like the images in this book and would like to investigate using them
for publishing, promotions or advertising, please visit our website www.practicalpictures.com
for more information.

Publisher: Joanna Lorenz
Editor: Joy Wotton
Jacket Designer: Nigel Partridge
Production Controller: Wendy Lawson

A CIP catalogue record for this book is available from the British Library.

Previously published as part of a larger volume, *The Drawing and Painting Course*

PUBLISHER'S NOTE
Although the advice and information in this book are believed to be accurate and true at the time of
going to press, neither the authors nor the publisher can accept any legal responsibility or liability for any
errors or omissions that may have been made nor for any inaccuracies nor for any loss, harm or injury
that comes about from following instructions or advice in this book.

Every effort has been made to credit the artists of the drawings and paintings
shown in the gallery sections of this book. We apologize for any omissions,
which will be rectified in future editions.

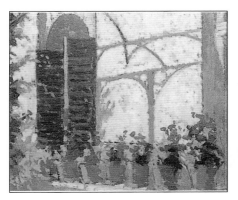
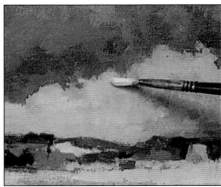
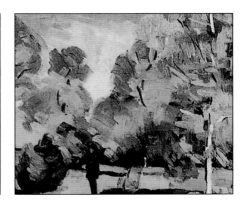

Contents

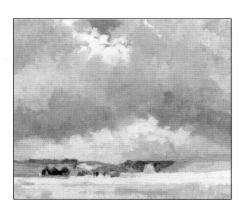
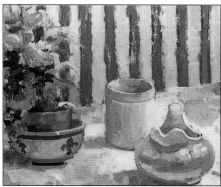
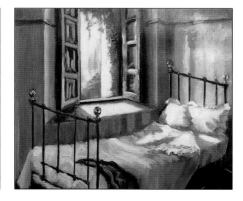

Introduction

Contrary to popular belief, oil paint is not a 'difficult' medium to work with. Quite the opposite; it is a perfect medium for the beginner because it is very easy to correct what you have done, either by wiping it out or by painting over it. Oil paint is a flexible medium, too; its smooth, buttery consistency, coupled with its slow drying time, means that it can be manipulated freely and extensively on the canvas to produce an infinite range of textures and effects. When oil paint is diluted with thinners it can be used to build delicate, translucent glazes that seem to glow with an inner light. Used straight from the tube it produces thick, rich impastos in which the texture of the paint and the mark of the brush become an integral part of the finished image.

Many people lead busy lives and can only spare a few hours a week to paint and draw. If this is your case, be patient with the results and don't expect instant success. Always remember that nothing of worth is achieved without effort. The projects in this book are designed to guide you through all the major techniques and help you take up the recreation of oil painting with great enthusiasm and confidence. Learn how to paint Alla Prima with the simple and delightful Spring Flowers project, or how to blend colours in the Still Life in Blue and White.

If your first attempts at painting are disappointing, don't get discouraged and give up – failure is a part of the learning process, and every time that you practise you will gain a little knowledge that you can incorporate into your next attempt. Even the great Masters experienced periods of frustration and self-doubt, but what made them great was that they never gave up; they battled on regardless, and when success came it was all the sweeter for being hard-won. You will soon discover that creating any kind of art is a continuous, never-ending process of

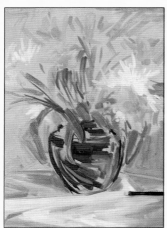

learning and discovery – which is what makes being an artist such a fascinating and rewarding occupation.

Today's artist is lucky in having a vast range of painting materials to choose from. Each medium possesses its own characteristics, and it is worth trying out some of them in order to discover their expressive potential and to determine whether or not they will suit your temperament and your way of working. Landscape painting is an important part of working in oils, and the projects on painting nature in Autumn Trees, and on mixing greens in A County Scene, contain many useful hints and tips.

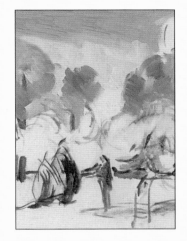

Many beginners think of oil painting as a challenging medium, but this book will guide you through its complexities. Painting in oils is an art form that can be manipulated freely and easily to create an infinite range of textures and effects.

Whatever medium, or media, you choose to work with, it is always advisable to acquire certain basic skills and practise with them before embarking on a major piece. In this book you will find an introduction to the materials, equipment and skills associated with this popular technique, backed up by detailed step-by-step demonstrations and examples of work by practising painters. I hope that it will help you to achieve creditable and attractive results and inspire you to keep going, even when the going gets tough.

Angela Gair

Materials and Equipment

Materials for oil painting can be expensive, so it is advisable to start out with the basic essentials and add extra colours, brushes and so on as you gain more experience.

PAINTS

Oil paints are sold in tubes and are available in two different grades: artists' and students'. Artists' colours are of better quality and this is reflected in the price. They are made from the finest pigments ground with a minimum of oil so their consistency is stiff, and the colours retain their brilliance well.

Students' colours are labelled with a trade name such as 'georgian' (Daler-Rowney) or 'Winton' (Winsor & Newton). These paints cost less because they contain less pure pigment and more fillers and extenders; they cannot provide the same intensity of colour as the artists' range. They are, however, fine for practising with. Some artists even combine the two types, using artists' paints for the pure, intense colours and students' paints for the earth colours, which are often just as good as in the artists' range.

Artist-quality paints vary in price according to the initial cost of the pigment. They are usually classified according to a 'series', typically from 1 (the cheapest) to 7 (the most costly). Student-quality colours are sold at a uniform price across the range.

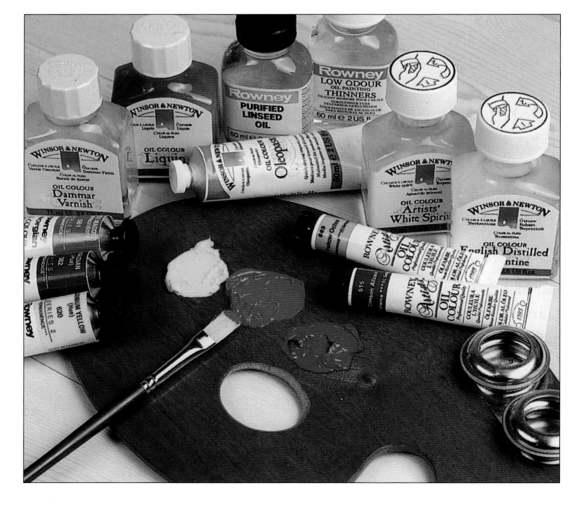

Right Some of the most popular mediums and diluents available for altering the consistency of oil paint. *From left to right*: dammar varnish, alkyd medium, impasto medium, purified linseed oil, low-odour thinners, white spirit, distilled turpentine. At the bottom right of the picture is a double dipper, which clips on to the palette and holds oil and turpentine separately so you can dip into them as you paint.

MEDIUMS AND DILUENTS

Oil paint can be used thickly, direct from the tube, but more often it needs to be diluted to make it easier to apply to the support. Paint may be thinned to the required consistency with a diluent such as turpentine or white spirit, or with a combination of a diluent and an oil or varnish – known as a medium.

Diluents

Used on its own, a diluent produces a matt finish and considerably accelerates the drying time of the paint. Always use double-distilled or rectified turpentine for painting purposes – ordinary household turpentine contains too many impurities and is not suitable.

If turpentine gives you a headache or irritates your skin, white spirit is a suitable alternative. It is also cheaper, has less odour, and stores without deteriorating. You can also obtain special low-odour thinners from art suppliers.

Mediums

There are various oils and resins that can be mixed with a diluent to add texture and body to your paint. The most commonly used painting medium is a mixture of linseed oil and turpentine, usually in a ratio of 60 per cent oil to 40 per cent turpentine. Linseed oil is used because it dries to a glossy finish that is resistant to cracking. However, be sure to buy either purified or cold-pressed linseed oil, because boiled linseed oil – the sort that is sold in DIY and hardware shops – contains impurities that cause rapid yellowing. If you want a thicker mixture that dries more quickly, you can

add a little dammar varnish to the turpentine and linseed oil.

Special ready-mixed painting mediums are available from art suppliers, designed variously to improve the flow of the paint, thicken it for impasto work, speed its drying rate, and produce either a matt or a gloss finish.

BRUSHES

Oil-painting brushes come in a wide range of sizes and shapes. Each makes a different kind of mark, but some are more versatile than others. Through experiment you will find which ones are best suited to your own painting style.

Below Here is a selection of the many oil-painting brushes available. A bristle brushes: fan, filbert, short flat, long flat. B synthetic brushes: round, flat, filbert. C mahl stick. D household decorator's brush – for applying primer to the support.

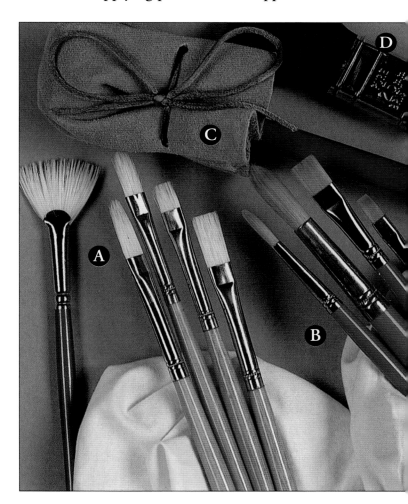

SAFETY PRECAUTIONS

Even small quantities of solvents and thinners can be hazardous if not used with care, because their fumes are rapidly absorbed through the lungs. When using solvents, always work in a well ventilated room and avoid inhalation. Do not eat, drink or smoke while working.

Bristle brushes

Stiff and hard-wearing, bristle brushes are good for moving the paint around on the surface and for applying thick dabs of colour. The best quality ones are made of stiff, white hog bristles with split ends that hold a lot of paint.

Sable brushes

Sable brushes are soft and springy, similar to those used in watercolour painting, but with longer handles. They are useful for painting fine details in the final layers of a painting and for applying thinly diluted colour. Sable brushes are expensive, however, and for oil painting some artists find synthetic brushes quite adequate.

Synthetic brushes

Synthetic brushes are an economical alternative to natural-hair brushes, and their quality has improved considerably in recent years. Synthetic brushes are hard-wearing and easily cleaned, but the cheaper ones lose their shape quickly.

Brush shapes

Rounds have long, thin bristles that curve inwards at the ends. This is the most versatile brush shape as it covers large areas quickly and is also good for sketching in outlines.

Flats have square ends and long bristles that hold a lot of paint. They are ideal for applying thick, bold colour and are useful for blending.

Brights are the same shape as flats, but with shorter, stiffer bristles that make strongly textured strokes. The stiff bristles are useful for applying thick, heavy paint to produce impasto effects.

Filberts are similar to flats, except that the bristles curve inwards at the end. Filberts are the most versatile brushes as they produce a wide range of marks.

Fan blenders are available in hog bristle, sable and synthetic fibre, and are used for blending colours together where a very smooth, highly finished effect is required.

Decorators' brushes are cheap, hard-wearing and useful for applying primer to the support prior to painting.

Brush sizes

Each type of brush comes in a range of sizes, from 00 (the smallest) to around 16 (the largest). Brush sizes are not standardized and can vary widely between brands. The brush size you choose will depend on the scale and style of your paintings. In general, it is better to start with medium to large brushes as they cover large areas quickly but can also be employed for small touches. Using bigger brushes also encourages a more painterly, generous approach.

Brush care

Good brushes are expensive, but if they are properly looked after they can last for several years. Clean your brushes at the end of every painting day, and never leave a brush soaking with the bristles touching the bottom of the container. First, remove the excess paint on a piece of newspaper, then rinse in white spirit and wipe on a rag. Wash under warm running water, soaping the bristles with a bar of household soap. Rub the soapy bristles in the palm of your hand so that the paint which has collected around the base of the ferrule is loosened. Rinse in warm water, shake dry, then smooth the bristles into shape. Leave the brushes to dry, bristle end up, in a jar. Always make sure brushes are dry before storing them in a closed container, or they may develop mildew.

PALETTES

Palettes for oil painting come in a variety of shapes, sizes and materials, designed to suit the artist's individual requirements. The best-quality palettes are made of mahogany ply, but fibreboard and melamine-faced palettes are perfectly adequate. Use as large a palette as you can, to allow your colours to be well spaced around the edge with plenty of room in the centre for mixing them together.

Thumbhole palettes

Thumbhole palettes come in a range of sizes and are designed to be held in the hand while painting at the easel. They have a thumbhole and indentation for the fingers, and the palette is supported on the forearm. There are three main shapes available: oblong, oval and the traditional kidney-shaped palette.

Preparing wooden palettes

Before they are used for the first time, wooden palettes should be treated by rubbing with linseed oil. This seals the wood and prevents it from sucking oil from the paint, causing it to dry out too quickly on the palette. It also makes the surface easier to clean after use. Rub a generous coating of the oil into both sides of the palette and leave it for several days until it has hardened and fully penetrated the grain.

Disposable palettes

Made of oil-proof paper, disposable palettes are useful for outdoor work and for those artists who hate the chore of cleaning up. They are sold in pads with tear-off sheets; some have a thumbhole.

Improvised palettes

Many artists prefer to use a 'home-made' palette which can be rested on a nearby surface. As well as saving you money, it allows you to choose any size, shape and material you like. Any smooth, non-porous material is suitable, such as a sheet of white formica, a glass slab with white or neutral-coloured paper underneath, or a sheet of hardboard sealed with a coat of paint. Old cups, jars and tins are perfectly adequate for mixing thin washes, and can be covered with plastic film between sessions to prevent the paint drying out.

SUPPORTS

The support is the surface on which you paint – whether canvas, board or paper. A support for oil painting must be prepared with glue size and/or primer to prevent it absorbing the oil in the paint; if too much oil is absorbed, the paint becomes underbound and may eventually crack.

Canvas

The most popular surface for oil painting is canvas, which has a unique responsiveness to the brush and plenty of tooth to hold the paint. Canvas is available in various weights and in fine, medium and coarse-grained textures. You can buy it either

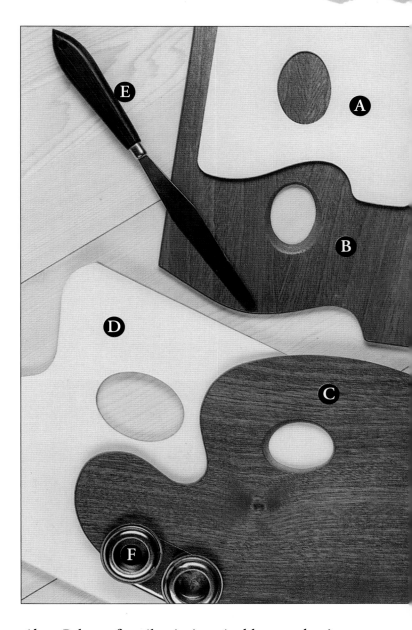

Above Palettes for oil painting. A oblong melamine. B oblong mahogany ply. C kidney-shaped 'studio' palette in mahogany ply. D pad of tear-off disposable palettes. A palette knife, E, is used for mixing paints together on the palette. A double dipper, F, will clip on to the side of your palette.

glued onto stiff board, ready-stretched and primed on a wooden stretcher frame, or in lengths from a roll. Prepared canvases are expensive and it is much cheaper to buy lengths of unprimed canvas and stretch and prime your own.

The weight of canvas is measured in ounces per square yard. The higher the number, the greater the density of threads and therefore the better the quality. The two main types of canvas available are linen and cotton.

Linen is considered the best canvas. It has a fine, even grain that is free of knots and a pleasure to paint on. Although expensive, it is very durable.

Cotton Good-quality cotton canvas, such as cotton duck, comes in 12oz and 15oz grades. It stretches well and is the best alternative to linen – at about half the price. Lighter-weight linen – at about half the price. Lighter-weight canvases are recommended for practice work only.

Boards and papers

Prepared canvas boards are relatively inexpensive and are ideal when trying out oils for the first time.

However, the cheaper ones have a rather mechanical texture and a slippery surface. **Hardboard,** which you can buy from builders' suppliers, is an excellent yet inexpensive support for oils. Most artists use the smooth side, as the rough side has a very insistent, mechanical texture. **Plywood, chipboard, MDF** (medium-density fibreboard) are also suitable for oil painting. Prepare the board with primer if you like a white

Below Oil paint can be applied to a wide range of supports. A stretched and primed canvas. B plywood. C hardboard. D oil sketching paper. E linen canvas. F cotton canvas (both of these need to be stretched and primed). G cardboard. H prepared canvas panel.

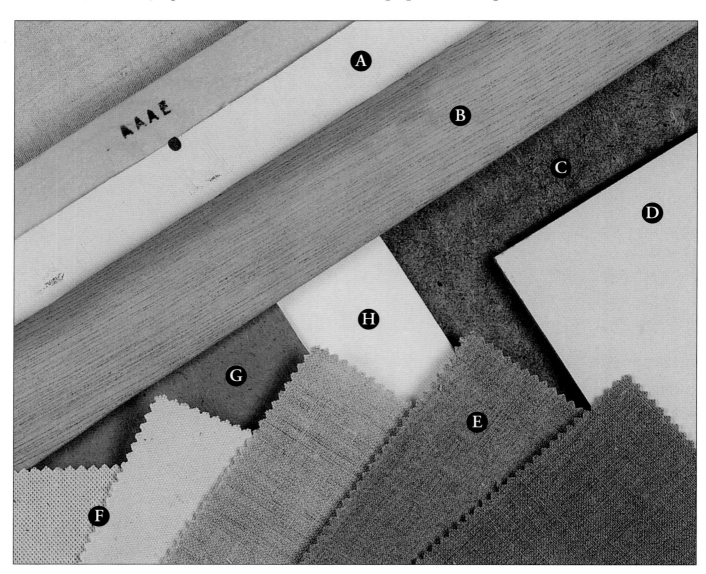

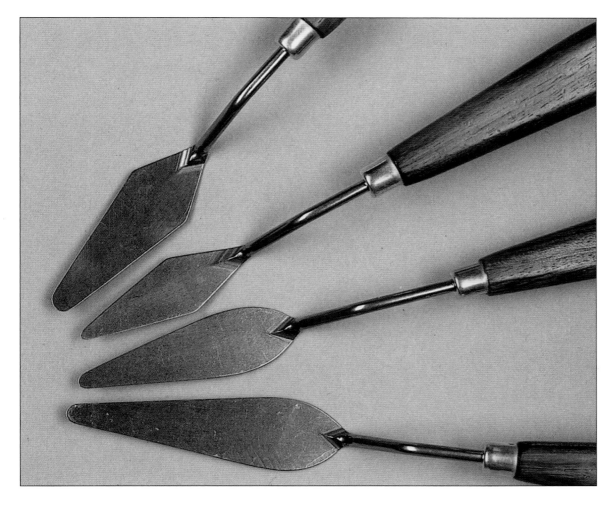

Left Painting knives come in a range of shapes and sizes. They are not an essential item unless you want to experiment with knife-painting techniques.

surface, or, if you prefer to work on a neutral mid-toned surface, simply apply a coat of glue size or PVA to the support.

Oil sketching paper is specially prepared for oil painting and is textured to resemble canvas weave. Available in pads with tear-off sheets, it is handy for outdoor sketches and practice work.

PAINTING ACCESSORIES

Painting in oils can be a messy business, so the most essential accessories that you will need are large jars or tins to hold solvents for cleaning brushes, and a good supply of cotton rags and newspaper! The following items are not essential, but some of them, such as palette knives, you will certainly find useful.

Painting knives have flexible blades and cranked handles, and can be used instead of a brush to apply thick paint directly to the support.

Palette knives have a long, straight, flexible blade with a rounded tip. They are used for mixing paint on the palette and for scraping paint off the palette at the end of a working session.

Dippers are small open cups that clip onto the edge of your palette to hold mediums and thinners during painting. These are not essential – you can just as easily keep small jars of painting medium on a nearby surface.

Mahl stick This is useful for steadying your hand when painting small details or fine lines. It consists of a long handle made from bamboo, wood or metal, with a rubber or chamois cushion at one end. Hold the mahl stick so that it crosses the painting diagonally, with the padded end resting lightly on a dry section of the work, or on the edge of the canvas. You can then rest your painting arm on the stick to steady yourself as you paint. You can make your own mahl stick from a length of dowelling or garden cane with a bundle of rags tied to one end.

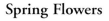

The Projects

Practical text and clear step-by-step photographs will lead you through the ten projects in this book and the different techniques involved in the art of painting in oils. Each project clearly explains the materials and oil paints you will need, plus expert guidance on the techniques used. With helpful hints and examples on every page, this book is as indispensable as paints, brushes and canvas in any artists' studio.

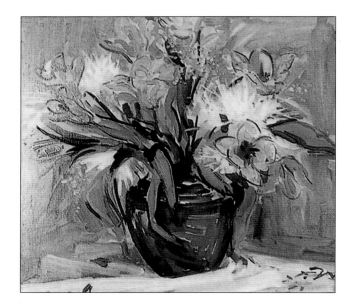

Spring Flowers   19

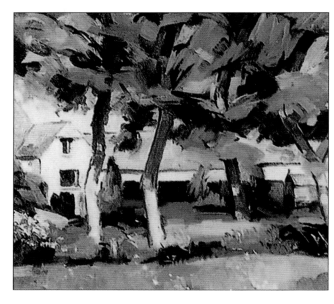

A Country Scene   34

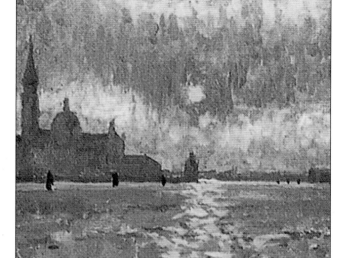

Venice, Evening   26

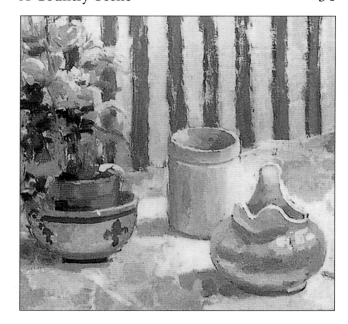

Still Life in Blue and Whites   42

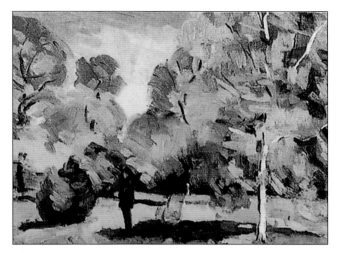

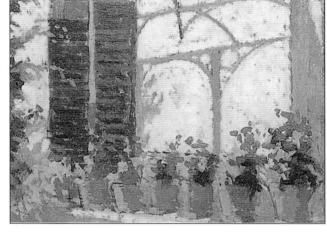
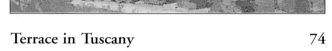

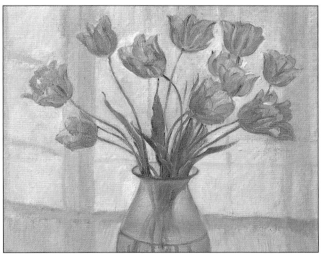

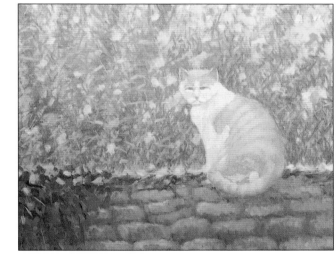

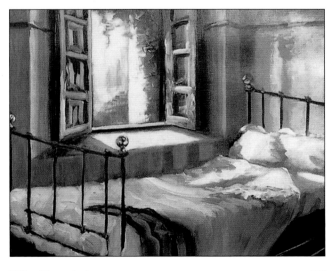

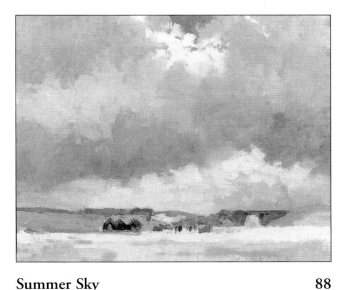

Painting Alla Prima

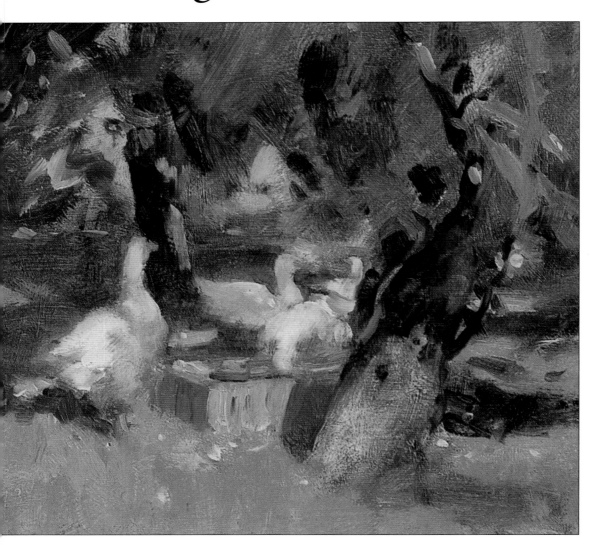

Trevor Chamberlain
ERIC'S GEESE
The artist had to work quickly to capture this delightful scene before the light changed and the geese wandered off. By using thinned paint and rapid, wet-in-wet brushstrokes, and by working on a small scale, he was able to complete the picture in about two hours.

Alla prima is an Italian expression meaning 'at the first'. It describes a technique in which a painting is completed rapidly in a single session, as opposed to the 'traditional' method of working up the image layer by layer over an extended period.

The alla prima method is often used by artists when painting outdoors directly from the subject, where speed is essential in order to capture the fleeting effects of light and movement in the landscape. In alla prima painting there is usually little or no initial underpainting, although artists sometimes make a rapid underdrawing in charcoal or thinned paint to act as a compositional guide. Each patch of colour is laid down more or less as it

will appear in the final painting, or worked wet-into-wet with adjacent colours; the main idea is to capture the essence of the subject in an intuitive way using vigorous, expressive brush strokes and minimal colour mixing.

Alla prima painting requires a confident approach. It is, of course, possible to scrape away and rework unsuccessful areas of a painting, but the danger is that some of the freshness and spontaneity will be lost. It is therefore important to start out with a clear idea of what you want to convey in your painting. Make a positive statement, and don't be tempted to include any unnecessary, cluttered detail.

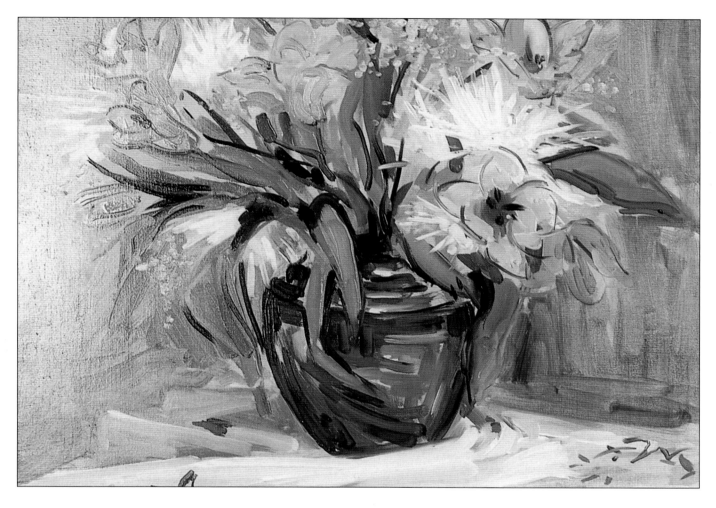

Spring Flowers

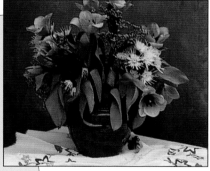

YOU WILL NEED

✓ Sheet of primed canvas or board, 18 x 14in (45.7 x 35.6cm)
✓ No. 2 round bristle brush
✓ No.2 filbert bristle brush
✓ No.8 filbert bristle brush
✓ No.10 filbert bristle brush
✓ Turpentine
✓ Linseed oil
✓ Clean rag

This painting was completed quickly, using a limited palette of colours. Bold, expressive brush-work gives rhythm to the composition, leading the eye around it from one area to another.

OIL PAINTS IN THE FOLLOWING COLOURS

- Naples yellow
- Chrome yellow
- Permanent rose
- Cadmium red
- Burnt sienna
- Cadmium green
- Yellow ochre
- Alizarin crimson
- Olive green
- French ultramarine
- Cobalt blue
- Cobalt violet
- Titanium white

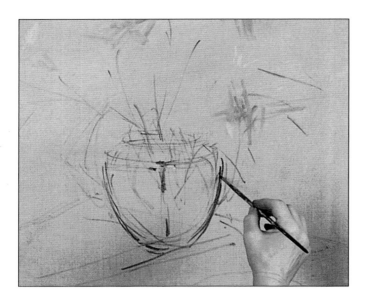

1 Prepare the canvas by tinting it the day before you start painting, so it has time to dry. Mix yellow ochre, French ultramarine and a little cadmium green, then dilute with lots of turpentine to make a very thin wash of pale grey-green. Rub the colour over the entire canvas area using a rag dampened with a little turpentine. Using a no. 2 filbert brush, lightly sketch in the main outlines of the composition with thin paint. Use French ultramarine for the vase, cobalt violet and titanium white for the tulips and cadmium green for the stalks. Hold your brush lightly, well back from the bristles, and draw with loose, fluid lines, feeling your way around the forms.

2 Establish the lightest tones in the composition – the white daisies and the highlights on the folds of the white tablecloth - using the 'rub-out' technique: fold a clean rag over your finger, dip it in turpentine, and remove some of the base colour, down to the bare canvas, as shown.

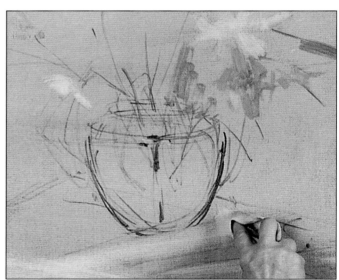

3 Now start to build up the composition as a whole, working on related areas simultaneously with small touches of thin paint. With a no. 10 flat brush, mix burnt sienna, yellow ochre and a little cadmium red to make a warm brown and loosely block in the background with broad strokes. Mix French ultramarine, alizarin crimson and white to create the shadows and folds in the tablecloth. Add strokes of ultramarine to the vase, following its curved form with your brush strokes. Paint the tulip leaves with cadmium green. For the darker leaves, add a touch of ultramarine and white to create a green with a hint of grey.

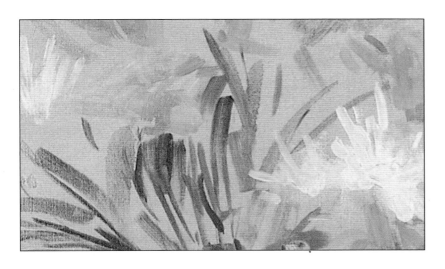

4 With a no. 8 filbert brush, work on the forms of the flowers. Use pure white, and white warmed with a little Naples yellow, for the daisies. Plot the light and dark tones of the tulips using various mixes of cobalt violet, cobalt blue, permanent rose and white. Apply the colours rapidly so you don't get bogged down in detail – concentrate instead on capturing the gestures of the petals.

Helpful Hint
IT'S IMPORTANT TO KEEP YOUR COLOURS FRESH AND UNSULLIED, SO RINSE YOUR BRUSHES FREQUENTLY IN A JAR OF WHITE SPIRIT.

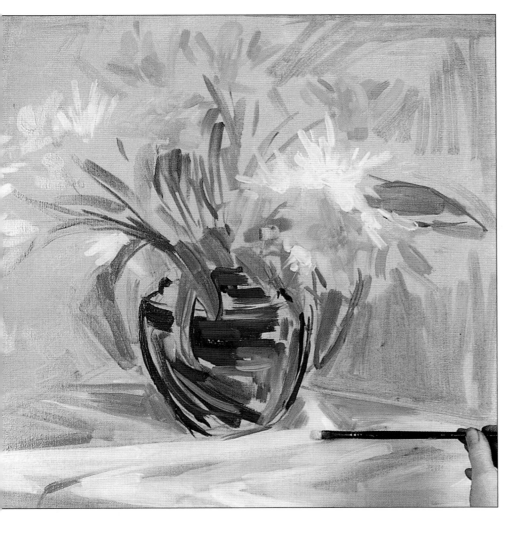

5 Now your painting is taking shape. From here on, mix your paint with turpentine and linseed oil to give it more body. Build up the reflections in the vase with French ultramarine, darkened with a touch of cobalt violet for the deepest tones, and cobalt blue and white for the highlights. Work on the folds in the tablecloth, deepening the shadows with a mix of burnt sienna and cobalt violet and adding white to the raised folds. Keep your brush moving and work on all the areas of the canvas.

6 Continue working on the vase with the same colours used in step 4. Add hints of cobalt violet to echo the colour of the tulips, and touches of pure white for the bright highlights. Let your brushstrokes describe the vase's rounded shape. Add tone and form to the leaves with a mixture of olive green and cadmium green, adding a little white for the highlights.

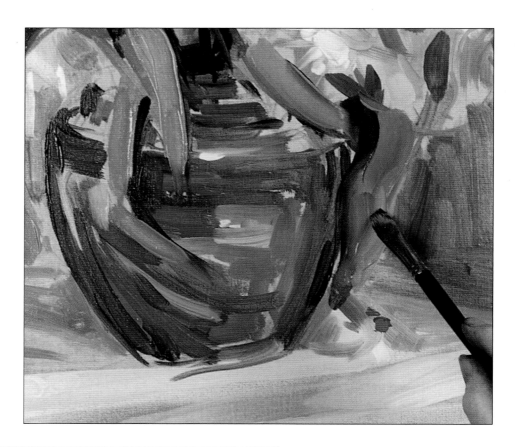

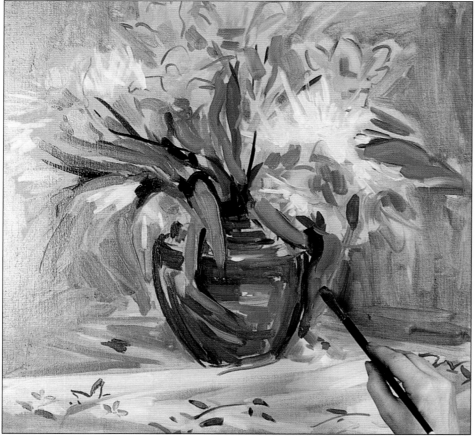

7 With a no. 2 round brush and cobalt violet, define the shapes of the tulips. With a no. 10 flat brush, fill in the background behind and between the flowers with a mix of burnt sienna, yellow ochre, chrome yellow and cadmium red. Suggest the embroidered flowers on the tablecloth using French ultramarine, cobalt blue and white for the petals, chrome yellow for the centres, and cobalt green darkened with cobalt blue for the stalks and leaves.

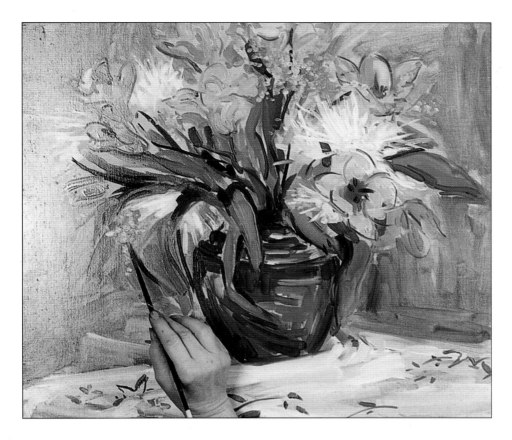

8 Add more white, mixed with a touch of cobalt blue, to the folds at the base of the vase. Using a no. 2 round brush, pick out the spiked petals of the daisies with pure white. Continue working on the tulips with mixtures of cobalt violet, cobalt blue, permanent rose and white, and touch in the stamens with pure cobalt violet. Let your brushstrokes follow the curved forms of the petals and allow the colours to mix wet-into-wet on the canvas. Mix cobalt violet and white and dot in the tiny statice flowers.

9 Stand back from the picture to see if there are any final adjustments that need to be made. Don't be tempted to add any unnecessary detail, however, otherwise you will lose the freshness and immediacy of your alla prima painting.

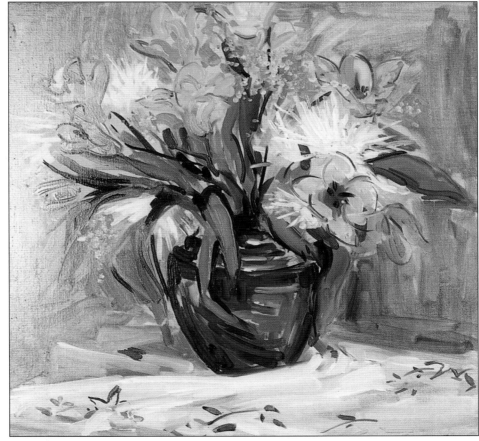

Toned Grounds

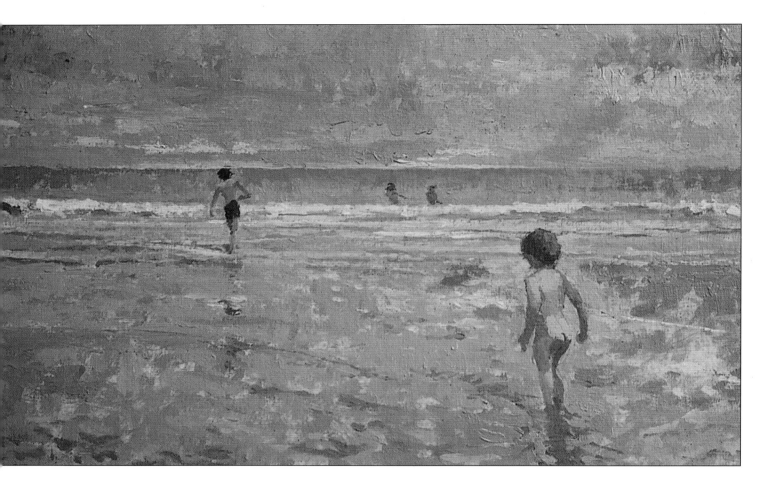

James Horton
BOYS BATHING AFTER A STORM
In this painting the artist has toned the canvas with a diluted earth colour. The toned ground breaks through the overlaid strokes, its warm colour providing a lively contrast with the cool greys of the sea and sky.

Once a canvas or board has been primed it can be given a wash of colour using thinned paint applied with a brush or rag. This is called a toned ground.

Toning the ground serves two purposes. First, it softens the stark white of the primed canvas or board, which can make it difficult to assess colours and tones accurately. A colour like red, for instance, may look quite dark when applied to a white canvas; but as the painting progresses that same red will be surrounded by other colours, and suddenly it looks much lighter. A neutral, mid-toned ground provides a more sympathetic surface on which to paint, and you can work out to the light and dark tones with equal ease.

Second, it patches of the coloured ground are allowed to show through the overpainting in places, they become an integral element of the painting and act as a harmonizing influence by tying the separate elements together.

Choosing the ground colour

The colour chosen for a toned ground will depend on the subject you are painting, but it is normally a neutral tone somewhere between the lightest and the darkest colours in the painting. The colour should be subtle and unobtrusive so that it does not overwhelm the colours in the overpainting.

Diluted earth colours such as Venetian red, raw sienna or burnt umber work very well, as do soft greys and greens. Some artists like a ground that harmonizes with the dominant colour of the subject; others prefer a ground which provides a quiet contrast. For instance, a warm red-brown enhances the greens in a landscape, while a soft ochre adds brilliance to the blues in a skyscape.

Applying the ground

Dilute the paint thinly with turpentine or white spirit and apply it with a large brush (a decorator's brush is useful). After a few minutes, rub with a clean rag, leaving a transparent stain of colour which is ready to paint on the following day. Alternatively, some artists prefer to apply the colour vigorously, leaving the brushmarks showing.

Always make sure the toned ground is completely dry before you paint over it. An oil ground usually takes around 24 hours to dry thoroughly, but if time is short you can use acrylic paint instead. Acrylic is an alkyd-based paint which is water soluble. It dries in minutes, allowing you to overpaint in oils straight away (though you should never apply acrylics over oils as this causes the picture surface to crack. This is because oils are more flexible and slow-drying than acrylics).

The other great advantage is that acrylic paint acts as both a sealing agent and a primer, so you don't need to size and prime the canvas as you would for oils (never apply acrylics on a ground which has been sized and primed for oils, however, as this may lead to eventual cracking of the paint film).

James Horton
COUNTRY SCENE
Here the toned ground has been chosen to harmonize, rather than contrast with, the colours in the painting. Although much of the ground is covered up, it has an important role to play, modifying the greens in the landscape and unifying the picture.

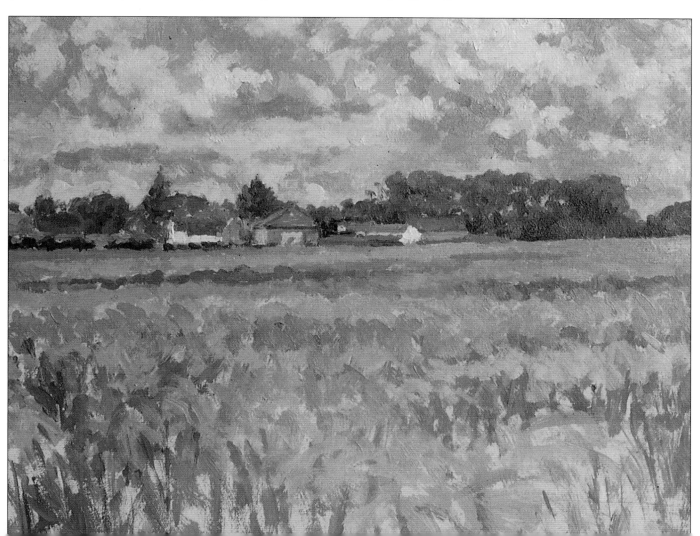

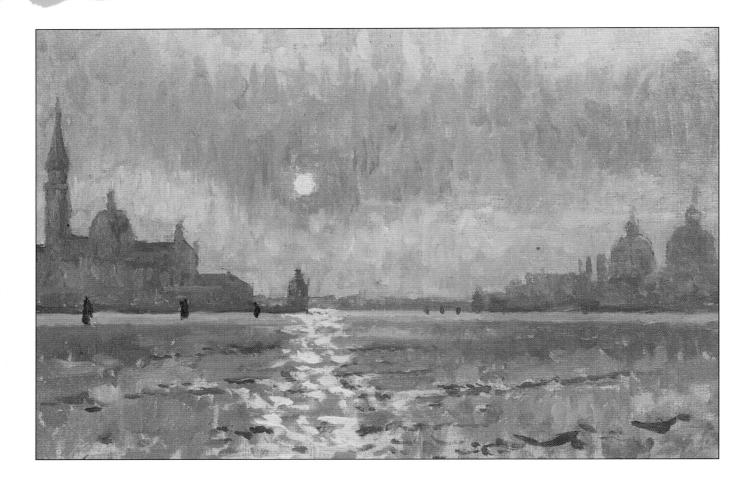

Venice, Evening

A carefully chosen toned ground can act as a mid tone and provide a link between disparate areas of colour. In this lovely painting, small patches of the umber ground remain exposed throughout the picture, their warm colour helping to unify the composition and enhancing the impression of the shimmering light of Venice at sunset.

OIL PAINTS IN THE FOLLOWING COLOURS

- *Raw umber*
- *Burnt sienna*
- *French ultramarine*
- *Cerulean*
- *Alizarin crimson*

- *Cadmium red*
- *Cadmium orange*
- *Lemon yellow*
- *Titanium white*
- *Ivory black*

YOU WILL NEED
- ✓ *Canvas board, 14 x 9¹/₂in (35.6 x 24.2cm)*
- ✓ *No. 2 round sable brush*
- ✓ *No. 5 round bristle brush*
- ✓ *1¹/₂in (38mm) decorating brush*
- ✓ *Turpentine*
- ✓ *Linseed oil*
- ✓ *Dammar varnish*

1 Cover the whole surface of the canvas board with a transparent wash of raw umber, diluted to a thin consistency with turpentine. Use a 1¹/₂in (38mm) decorating brush for this. The aim is to knock back the stark whiteness of the primed board and establish a warm mid tone against which you can judge the lighter and darker tones. Leave to dry overnight. Dilute raw umber and burnt sienna with turpentine and sketch in the main outlines of the scene, including the orb of the sun, with a no. 2 round sable brush.

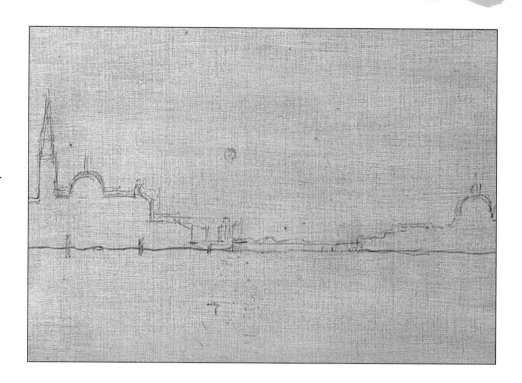

Helpful Hint
WHEN PAINTING LANDSCAPES, AVOID PLACING THE HORIZON LINE IN THE CENTRE OF THE CANVAS AS THIS EFFECTIVELY CUTS THE PICTURE IN HALF.

2 From here on, mix your colours with a little medium, consisting of equal amounts of linseed oil and dammar varnish and twice the amount of turpentine. Mix a warm grey from raw umber, French ultramarine and alizarin crimson and loosely touch in the buildings in the distance with a no. 5 round bristle brush. Then mix a vibrant, turquoise grey with ultramarine, white and a little lemon yellow and paint the upper part of the sky with random brushstrokes, letting the ground show through.

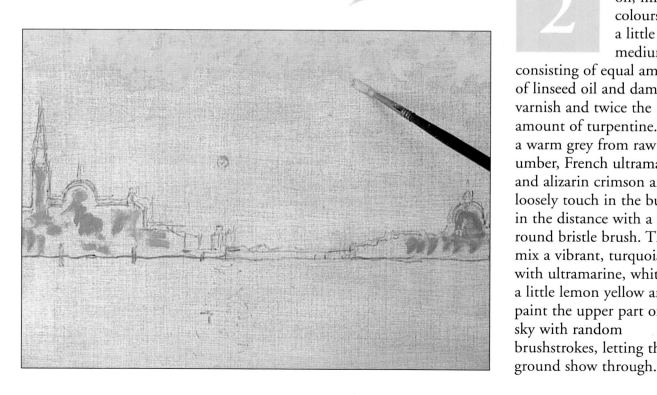

27

3 With the same brush, continue painting the sky, starting beneath the first band of colour with a combination of ultramarine, alizarin crimson, titanium white and a tiny spot of ivory black. As you work down towards the horizon, add more alizarin and a little more white to the mix so that the sky gradually takes on a warm, violet hue. Again, apply the colours with loosely spaced marks, leaving plenty of the ground colour showing through.

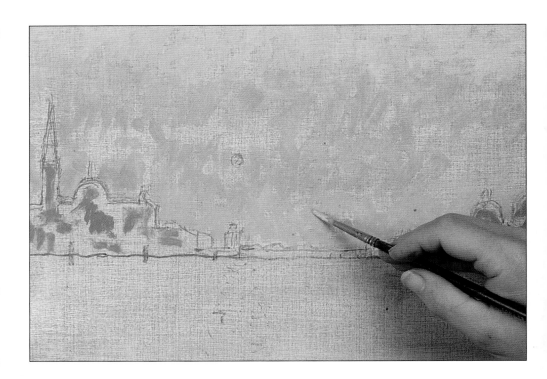

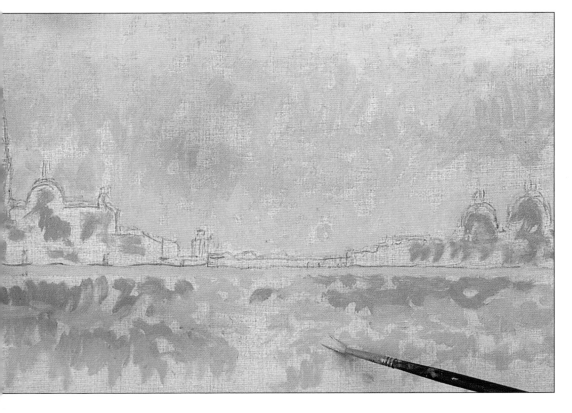

4 Start to work up the greenish tones in the water, leaving a 'pathway' for the sun's reflection. The basic colours are ultramarine, lemon yellow, cerulean and white – mix these in different combinations to give a range of greenish greys. For example, add more blue for the darker, cooler greens and more yellow or white for the lighter, warmer hues. Suggest light shining on the distant water with a band of pale green.

5 Mix lemon yellow, cadmium orange and white and paint the brilliant orb of the sun. Use fairly thick paint so that it catches the light. Then mix ultramarine, alizarin and white and use this to create a cool 'halo' of blue-grey around the sun, using loose strokes that follow a circular shape. This is an example of how one colour can be influenced by neighbouring colours; the yellow sun appears more brilliant in contrast with the darker tone of grey surrounding it.

6 Paint the group of buildings on the left of the picture with soft blue-violet greys mixed from various amounts of ultramarine, alizarin, black and white (make use of the greys already mixed on your palette). Instead of 'filling in' with a flat layer of paint, apply small strokes and dabs of subtly modulated colour. Allow small patches of the toned ground to show through the strokes; this gives a soft effect that suggests hazy evening light gently enveloping the scene.

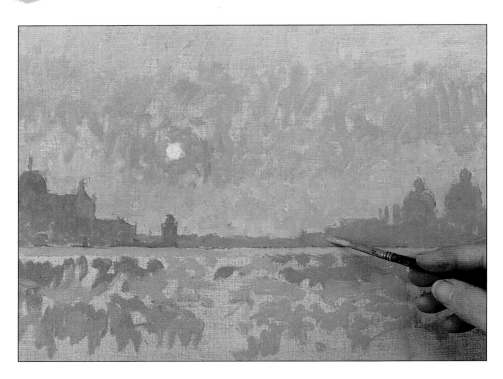

7 Suggest the soft rosy glow in the sky near the horizon with a mixture of cadmium red, lemon yellow and lots of white, applied with loose strokes. Now fill in the rest of the buildings, which lie behind those on the left. Use the same mix as in step 6, adding more white to lighten the tone and push the buildings back in space.

8 Mix lemon yellow, cadmium orange and white and paint the sun's broken reflection on the water. Use a no. 2 round sable brush to make rhythmic strokes and ticks that suggest the gentle lapping of the water. To enhance the effect of space and perspective, make these strokes smaller and more closely spaced in the distance, as well as lighter in tone.

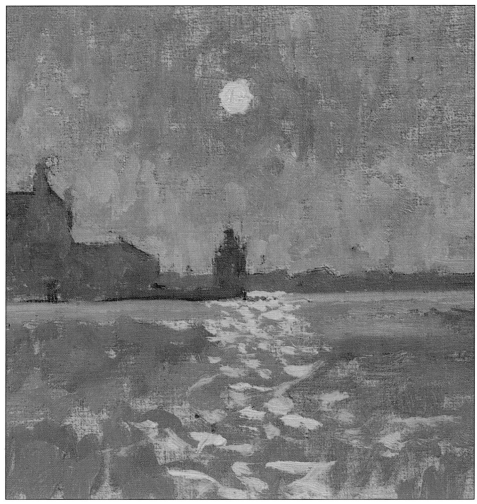

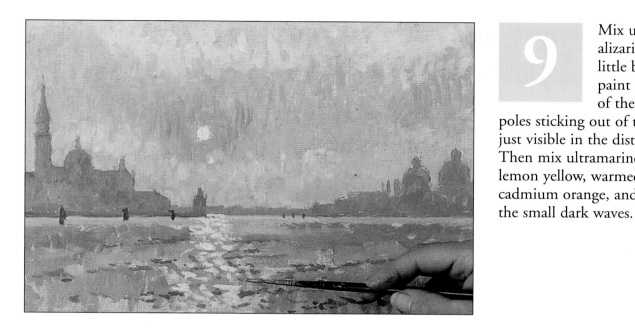

9 Mix ultramarine, alizarin and a little black to paint the tops of the wooden poles sticking out of the water, just visible in the distance. Then mix ultramarine and lemon yellow, warmed with cadmium orange, and touch in the small dark waves.

10 Look for the tonal balances of colour and make sure nothing jumps out at you – the effect should be one of hazy evening light. Any sharp divisions of colour can be softened and blended by gently hatching over them with a no. 2 round sable brush, to produce atmospheric blends and veils of colour.

Helpful Hint
WHITE IS USED A LOT IN OIL-PAINTING MIXTURES, SO IT IS MORE ECONOMICAL TO BUY A LARGE TUBE OF IT.

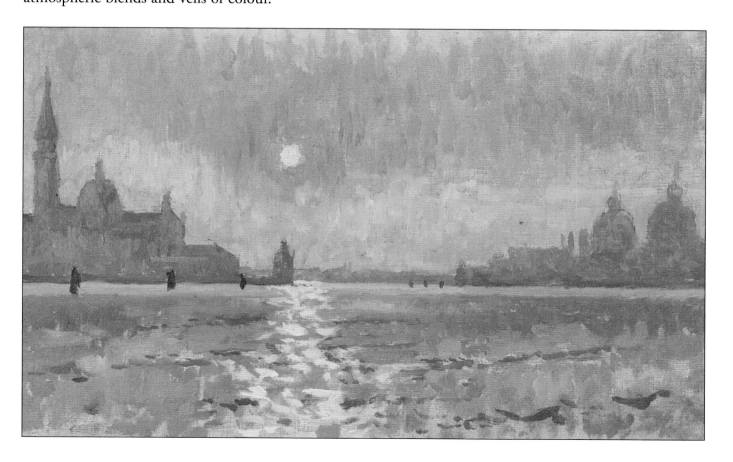

Mixing Greens

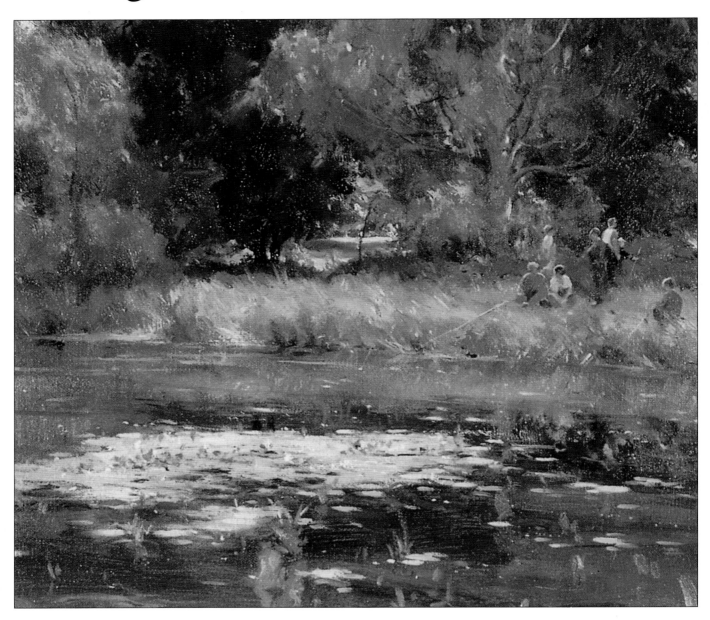

David Curtis
FISHING BY THE LAKE
A rich variety of greens is woven throughout this painting. Note how a sense of depth is created by using warm greens in the foreground and cooler greens in the distance.

Green is often the dominant colour in landscapes, but that green can vary enormously from almost blue to near yellow. Before you start to mix paint, it is worthwhile to go out and observe the landscape, comparing the different greens to each other. You will find that on a bright day, for instance, sunlit areas of grass and foliage are a warm, yellowish green, while those greens in shadow appear cooler and bluer. And, if you look towards the horizon, then you will see that the greens of trees, fields and hills appear progressively cooler, bluer and paler in tone as they recede into the distance.

Where many inexperienced painters go wrong is in painting an entire landscape using ready-mixed greens straight from the tube, and then simply adding white or black to make them lighter or darker. Because there aren't enough contrasts of light and dark tone and warm and cool colour, the result is a flat, monotonous painting with no feeling of light.

If you want to paint realistic landscapes, it is worth learning how to mix more lively greens, and there are two ways in which you can do this: using tube greens modified with other colours, and mixing your own greens from blues and yellows.

Modifying tube greens

There are several greens available ready-mixed in tubes, but most of them are too intense, not like the soft greens of nature. However, tube greens are excellent when modified by the addition of other colours on your palette. For example, viridian is an intense, cold green that looks unnatural in its pure state. But by adding red, yellow or orange to it, it is possible to create a whole range of life-like greens.

Mixing blues and yellows

Blues and yellows mixed together give an even wider range of rich and subtle greens that can be varied from light to dark, bright to muted and warm to cool. Such greens can be further adjusted by adding a third colour, such as a touch of red if the green is too bright and you want to tone it down a little.

Discover for yourself the value of mixing your own greens. Take three blues – cerulean, cobalt and ultramarine – and three yellows-lemon, cadmium and ochre. Add each of the yellows to each of the blues, and you instantly have nine different greens, ranging from bright, leafy hues to warm, rich tones. Start with a 50:50 mix, then see what happens when you alter the proportions of each colour in turn: adding more blue creates darker, cooler greens, while more yellow creates brighter, warmer greens. You can extend the possibilities even further by experimenting with adding touches of earth colours such as raw sienna or raw umber to make even richer greens.

Warm and cool greens

Colours are classed as being either 'warm' or 'cool' in temperature, and in general blue is regarded as cool, and yellow as warm. However, within this broad definition, some blues are warmer or cooler than others, and the same goes for yellows. French ultramarine contains a hint of red, so is warmer than cerulean; lemon yellow has a green cast, so is cooler than cadmium yellow.

Bear this in mind when mixing greens for your landscapes; it you want a cool green for painting shadowy foliage, it makes sense to choose a cool blue such as winsor blue and a cool yellow such as lemon yellow. If you want a warm, rich green for sunlit foliage, try a blend of ultramarine and cadmium yellow. When mixing colours, bear in mind that some colours are strong and others weak. A little cadmium yellow, for instance, goes a long way, so add it in small amounts.

The colour swatches below demonstrate just some of the colour combinations that will give you a wide range of lively and expressive greens.

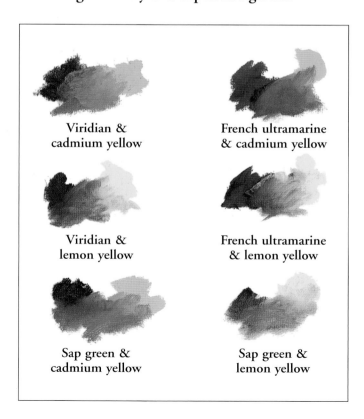

Viridian & cadmium yellow	French ultramarine & cadmium yellow
Viridian & lemon yellow	French ultramarine & lemon yellow
Sap green & cadmium yellow	Sap green & lemon yellow

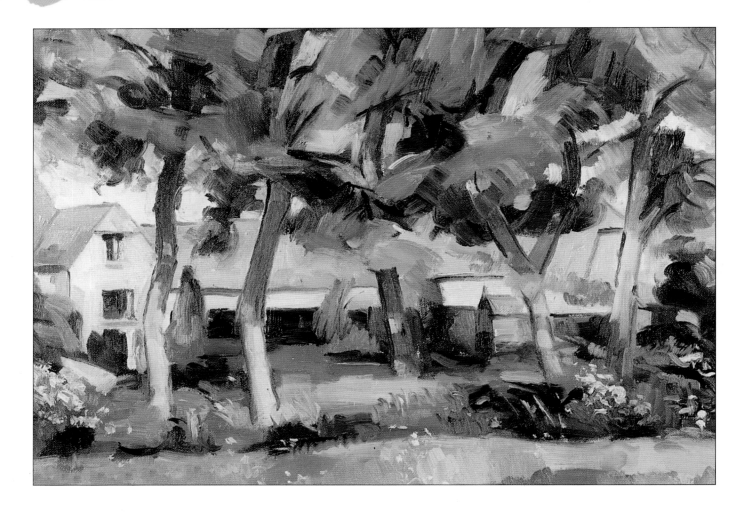

A Country Scene

In this lively painting the artist has succeeded in mixing a wide range of foliage greens, from cool blue shades to vibrant yellow hues. He used a limited palette of colours, mixing greens from various blues and yellows and modifying tube greens with other colours.

OIL PAINTS IN THE FOLLOWING COLOURS

- *Lemon yellow*
- *Spectrum yellow*
- *Yellow ochre*
- *Venetian red*
- *Cobalt violet*

- *Chrome oxide green*
- *Permanent green*
- *French ultramarine*
- *Cerulean*
- *Titanium white*

YOU WILL NEED

- ✓ *Sheet of canvas board, 20 x 16in (50.8 x 40.6cm)*
- ✓ *Nos. 2, 5 and 10 flat bristle brush*
- ✓ *No.4 filbert bristle brush*
- ✓ *Distilled turpentine*
- ✓ *Purified linseed oil*
- ✓ *Charcoal*

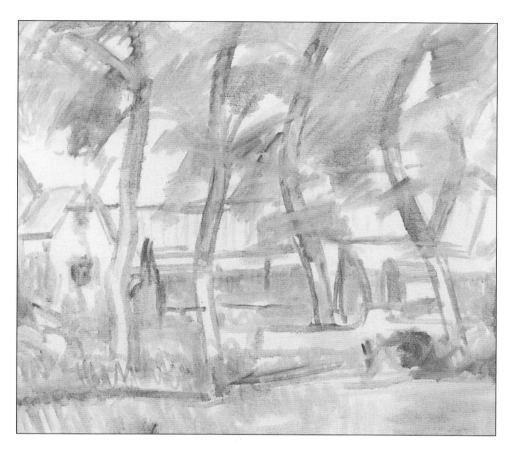

1 Sketch in the main outlines of the composition with charcoal. Dilute some chrome oxide green with turpentine so it flows easily and, with a no. 4 filbert bristle brush, loosely paint in the main areas, using the charcoal marks as a guide.

2 Mix a cool green from permanent green, French ultramarine and chrome oxide green, adding a little linseed oil to the turpentine to make the paint more workable. With a no. 10 flat brush, work across the canvas using broad strokes to block in the darkest areas in the pine trees and the cast shadows on the grass. Vary the direction of your brush strokes to convey the direction of growth of the branches.

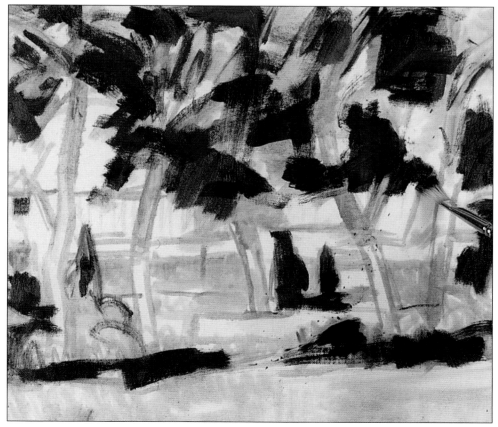

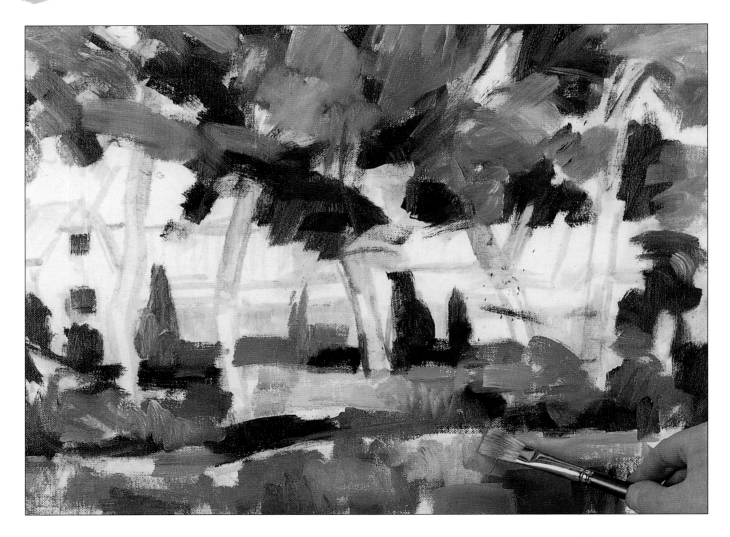

3 Now bring in some yellow ochre, lemon yellow and spectrum yellow, mixing them with the greens and blues in varying proportions to make a range of warmer, lighter greens for the sunlit foliage and grass. Partially blend the colours on the canvas and vary the proportions of the colours in your mixes, adding more yellows to warm up the sunny greens and more blue to cool down the shadowy greens. Add a little titanium white to the palette to introduce light to the picture, but not too much as it tends to make the colours go dull and chalky.

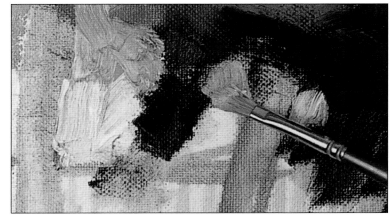

4 Mix a pale blue from cerulean and titanium white and paint the sky, cutting in around the foliage. Paint the clouds with white and a hint of cerulean. Use a no. 5 flat brush for the broad areas and a no. 2 for the smaller patches.

5 With a no. 4 filbert brush, block in the pinks and browns of the buildings in the background with broad strokes. Use a base mixture of venetian red and titanium white, adding some yellow ochre and spectrum yellow for the warm-coloured roofs and some cobalt violet and cerulean for the slate roof in the middle.

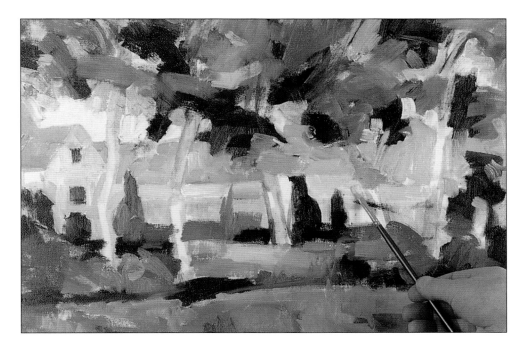

Helpful Hint
TRY TO INTRODUCE TOUCHES OF SIMILAR COLOUR
IN DIFFERENT PARTS OF THE PICTURE. THIS WILL
CREATE A SATISFYING, HARMONIOUS EFFECT.

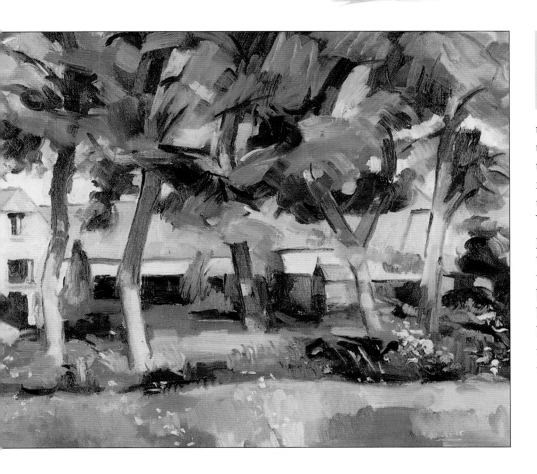

6 The canopy of foliage casts violet-tinged shadows onto the upper parts of the tree trunks; paint these using mixtures of cobalt violet, ultramarine and a little Venetian red, varying the proportions of the colours to create light and dark tones. Now that you have blocked in most of the base colours, you can begin to work over them to develop contrasts of tone and texture.

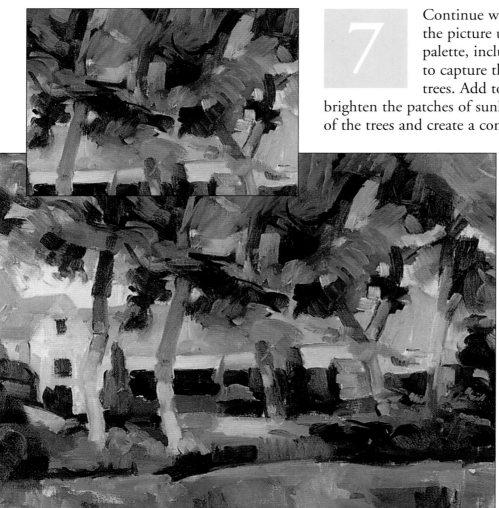

7 Continue working on the green areas of the picture using all the colours on your palette, including a little violet and blue to capture the really deep tones in the trees. Add touches of spectrum yellow to brighten the patches of sunlit foliage at the outer edges of the trees and create a contrast with the dark tones in the shadows. In the detail (left) you can see how the artist has partially blended his colours on the canvas, wet-into-wet, and varied the angle of his brush to create lively marks that give a sense of movement to the foliage.

Helpful Hint
GREENS CAN BE LIGHTENED WITH WHITE OR YELLOW AND DARKENED WITH BLACK, BLUE OR RED. WHITE MAKES SOME COLOURS APPEAR CHALKY, AND BLACK CAN HAVE A DEADENING EFFECT.

8 Go over the buildings with a no. 2 flat brush, putting in outlines and the shadows under the eaves with a mixture of cobalt violet and ultramarine. Darken the shadows on the tree trunks with the same colour; this contrast of dark tone against the lighter tones of the buildings helps to create a sense of space and depth in the picture.

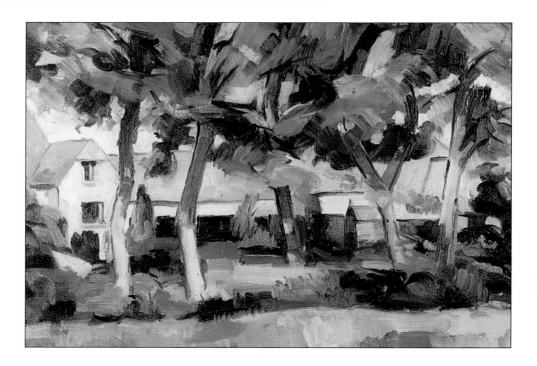

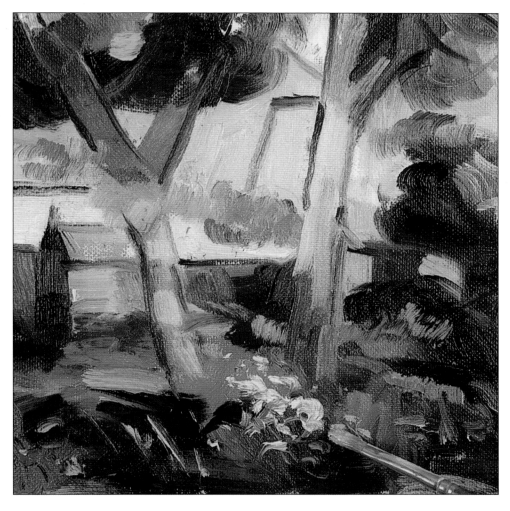

9 Now start adding the details, suggesting the rose bushes in the foreground with dabs of venetian red and titanium white. Roll the well-loaded brush over the surface to deposit the paint – this technique is known as scumbling.

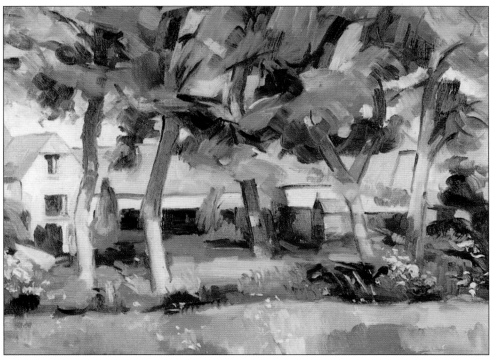

10 The final picture gives a lively impression of sunlight breaking through the shady pine trees. Notice the variety of greens the artist has used, from cool blue-greens through to vibrant yellow-greens. A refreshing note of contrast is provided by the warm, reddish tones of the buildings in the background.

Blending

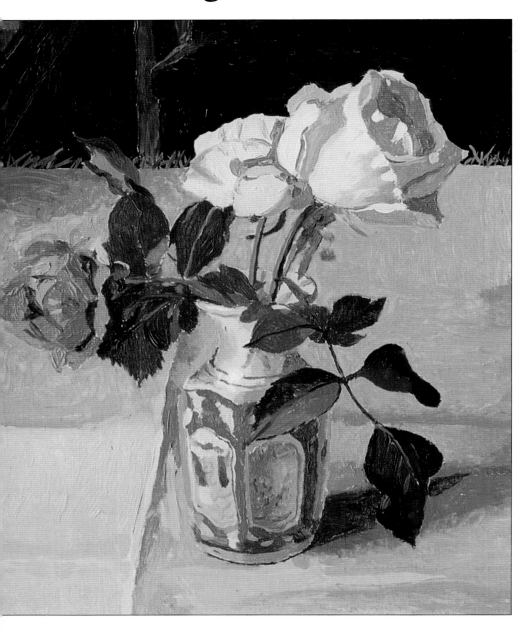

Blending is a means of achieving soft gradations between adjacent tones or colours by brushing them together where they meet, wet-into-wet. Oil paint lends itself readily to the blending technique because its soft, buttery consistency and slow drying time mean the paint can be freely manipulated on the painting surface.

Subjects

Smooth gradations of colour are used in painting to render specific materials and surface qualities such as soft fabrics, skin tones, flowers, fruits and the reflective surfaces of metal and glass. They are also used to describe certain atmospheric impressions found in the landscape, such as skies and clouds, fog and mist, and reflections in water. In landscapes and seascapes, an impression of space, light and atmosphere can be created by softening the line where sky and horizon meet.

Techniques

The techniques of fusing colour fall between two extremes. On the one hand you can blend the colour with your brush so smoothly and silkily that the brushstrokes are imperceptible even when viewed close-up. At the other extreme it is possible to roughly knit the colours together so that the brushmarks remain visible at close quarters; when viewed at a distance the colours appear to merge together, yet they retain a lively quality because they are only partially blended.

Jeremy Galton
ROSES IN BLUE VASE
Too many sharply focused edges can make delicate subjects look hard and brittle. This floral still life shows how a sensitive handling of tones and edges can suggest form without overstatement. Notice how most of the tones and colours are blended wet-into-wet, with just a few touches here and there to bring the picture into focus.

Brushes

Any type of brush can be used for blending, depending on your style of painting. Some artists use stiff-bristled brushes so as to retain the liveliness of the brushstrokes. Others prefer to use softhair brushes to achieve very smooth, perfect gradations. Special brushes called 'fan blenders' – they have long hairs arranged in a fan shape – are specially adapted for smooth blending; work over the edge between two tones or colours using a gentle sweeping motion until a smooth, imperceptible blend is achieved.

David Curtis
HOT AUGUST EVENING BY THE RIVER
Colour, composition and brushwork all contribute to the peaceful atmosphere of this pastoral scene. A harmonious palette of warm colours sets the mood; and the smoothly blended brushstrokes capture the hazy light of a summer evening.

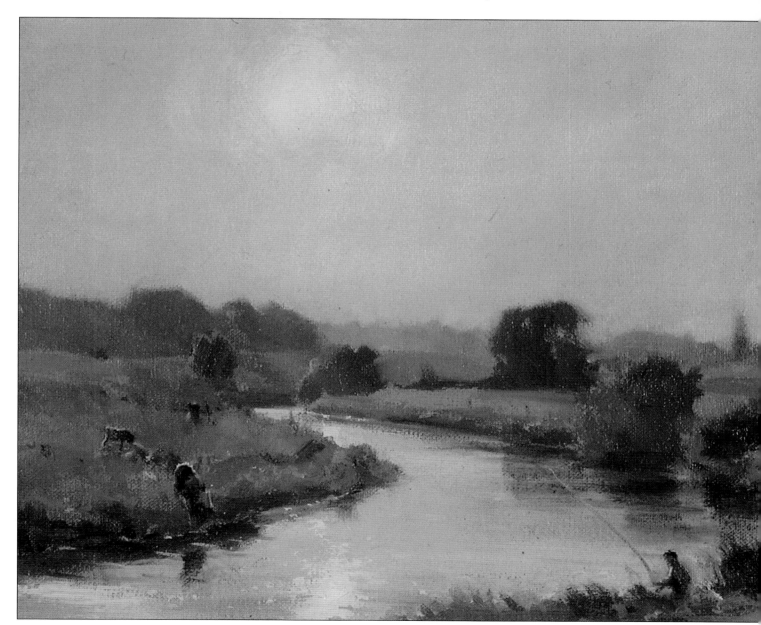

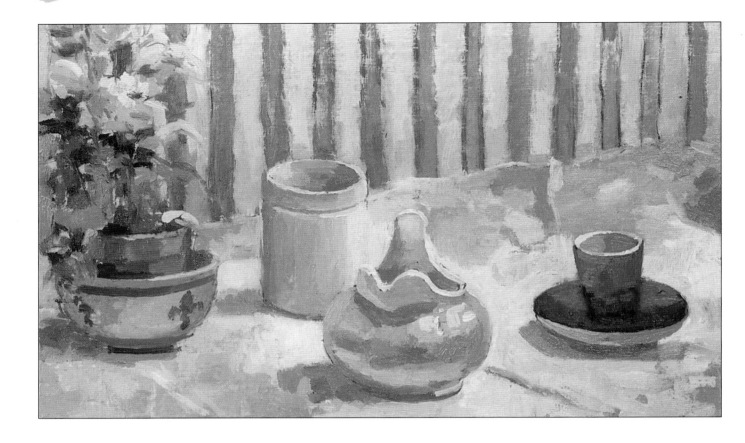

Still Life in Blue and White

In this painting the artist has blended his colours softly into one another, wet-into-wet, producing gentle gradations of tone and hue that describe the rounded forms of the pots and bowls, and give them solidity and weight.

OIL PAINTS IN THE FOLLOWING COLOURS

- *French ultramarine*
- *Cerulean*
- *Yellow ochre*
- *Naples yellow*
- *Veridian*
- *Raw umber*

- *Burnt sienna*
- *Cadmium red*
- *Alizarin crimson*
- *Titanium white*
- *Ivory black*

YOU WILL NEED

✓ *Sheet of primed canvas or board, 12 x 9in (30.5 x 22.8cm)*
✓ *1½in (38mm) decorating brush*
✓ *No. 5 round bristle brush*
✓ *No. 2 round sable brush*
✓ *No. 4 round sable brush*
✓ *No. 4 filbert bristle brush*
✓ *Refined linseed oil*
✓ *Distilled turpentine*
✓ *Dammar varnish*

1 Start by staining your canvas or board with a thin wash of cadmium red mixed with a little French ultramarine. Use a 1¹/₂in (38mm) decorating brush to spread the colour over the surface in wide sweeps. Leave to dry overnight. Then sketch in the main outlines of the composition with a no. 2 round sable brush and burnt sienna, thinned to a watery consistency with turpentine.

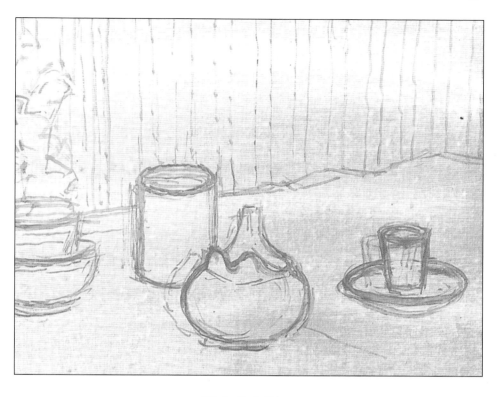

Helpful Hint
THE ARTIST MIXED HIS PAINTS WITH EQUAL
PROPORTIONS OF LINSEED OIL AND DAMMAR
VARNISH, PLUS TWICE THE VOLUME OF TURPENTINE.
THE ADDITION OF DAMMAR VARNISH TO THE BASIC
TURPS AND OIL MEDIUM GIVES A RICH,
ENAMEL-LIKE QUALITY TO THE PAINT.

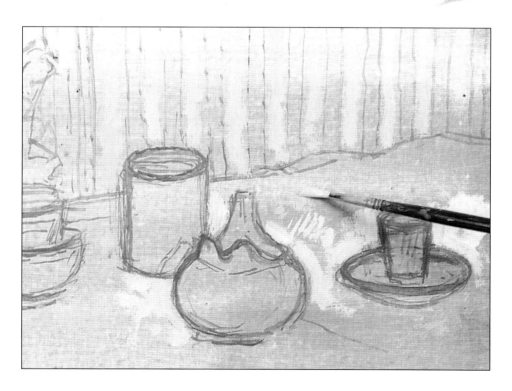

2 From this point, mix your colours with an oil medium (see Helpful Hint above) to make the paint more workable. Squeeze some titanium white onto your palette and blend tiny touches of yellow ochre and raw umber into it, just to take the edge off the white. With a no. 5 round bristle brush, roughly block in the white stripes on the wallpaper and start to paint the white cloth, twisting and turning the brush to create lively strokes.

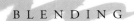

3 Mix two blues for the blue stripes on the wallpaper: French ultramarine and white for the darker, warmer stripes, and cerulean and white for the cooler, lighter stripes behind the plant. Use fairly dry paint and keep them quite 'sketchy' in feel so that they stay in the background – if they are too clearly defined they will leap forward in the picture plane.

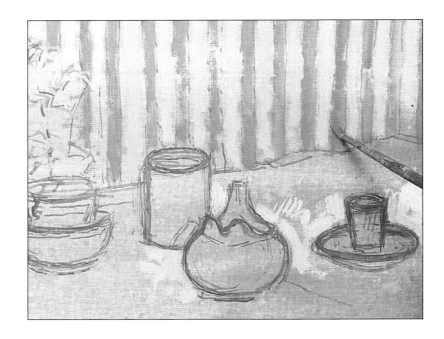

4 Establish the broad areas of light and shade on the china bowl and block them in, using a mix of French ultramarine, ivory black, alizarin crimson and white for the lighter tone, and a darker mix with yellow ochre added for the dark tone. Do the same for the terracotta plant pot, using various proportions of cadmium red, burnt sienna and white to create the light, dark and mid tones. Block these in quite broadly, making no attempt to blend the colours at this stage.

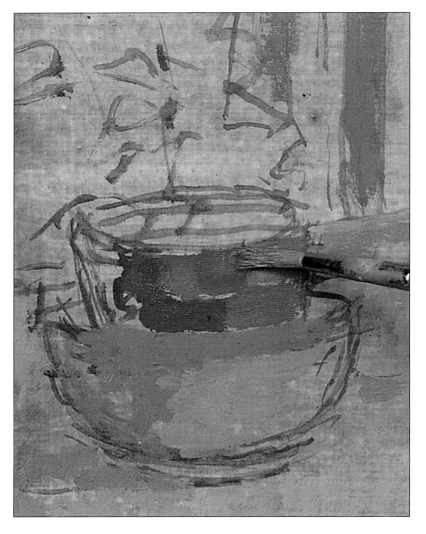

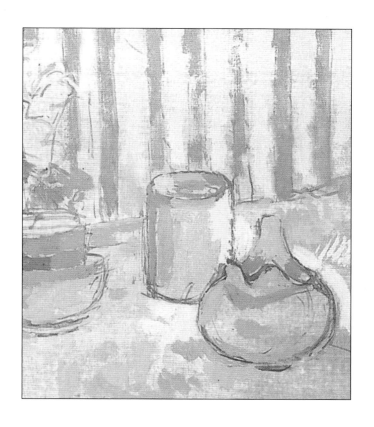

5 Rather than committing to one area in detail, move around the picture putting in touches of colour so that you can assess how the various tones and colours are balancing each other. Paint the shadows on the jug (pitcher) and jar with yellow ochre and raw umber, then block in the mid tones using the greys mixed in step 4. Add touches of pale mauve, mixed from ultramarine, alizarin, white and a hint of black, where colour is reflected onto the jug and jar from the pink cyclamen flowers. Mix Naples yellow and white for the highlight on the right side of the jar. Use the same colours to establish the soft shadows on the white cloth.

Helpful Hint
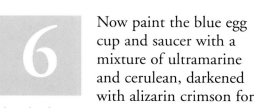
IF YOU FIND IT DIFFICULT TO ASSESS THE RELATIVE TONES IN YOUR SUBJECT, TRY LOOKING AT IT THROUGH HALF-CLOSED EYES. THIS CUTS OUT MUCH OF THE DETAIL, ALLOWING YOU TO SEE THE LIGHTS, DARKS AND MID TONES MORE CLEARLY.

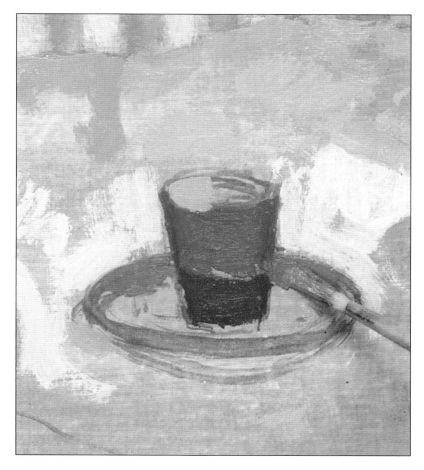

6 Now paint the blue egg cup and saucer with a mixture of ultramarine and cerulean, darkened with alizarin crimson for the shadow areas.

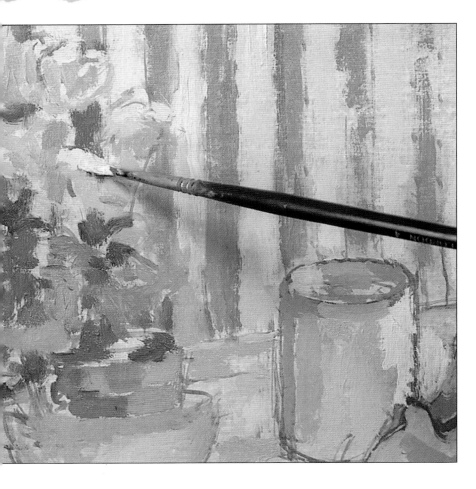

7 Switch to a no. 4 round sable brush and establish the main forms of the cyclamen plant. For the leaves, make up a series of warm and cool greens mixed from varying amounts of viridian, ultramarine, white, and grey from the palette. Do the same for the flowers, mixing warm and cool pinks from cadmium red (a warm red), alizarin crimson (a cool red) and white.

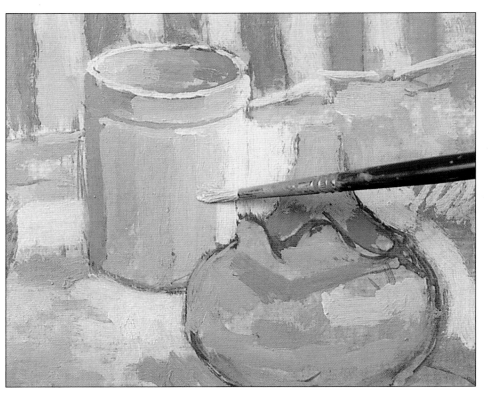

8 Use the same brush to paint the blue pattern on the china bowl with a mixture of ultramarine and white, darkened with a little alizarin crimson where the pattern turns into shadow.

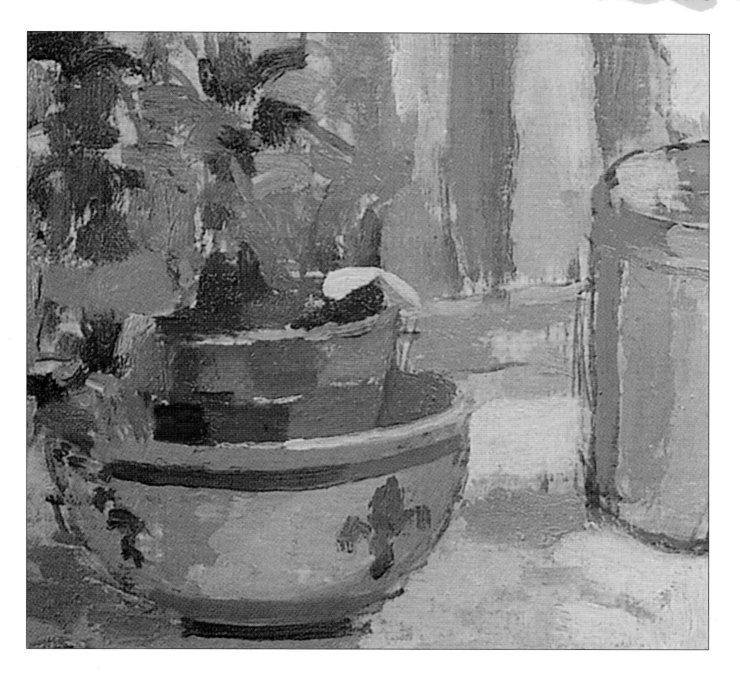

9 With everything in place and the broad tones and colours established, you can start to define the form and volume of the objects by blending the tones together to create smooth gradations. Working on the jar with the no. 4 round sable brush and the same colours used for the initial block-in, create a more even progression of tones from light to dark. Apply the colours wet-in-wet, slightly – but not too smoothly – blending the edge between one tone and the next. Mix white and a little Naples yellow for the highlight on the rim of the jar.

10 Continue to work around the painting, blocking in broad areas of tone and colour and then blending them together. Paint the greenish shadows inside the egg cup, and beneath the saucer, with a combination of yellow ochre plus a little black and white. Then use your Naples yellow and white mix to paint the highlit rims of the jug and the egg cup.

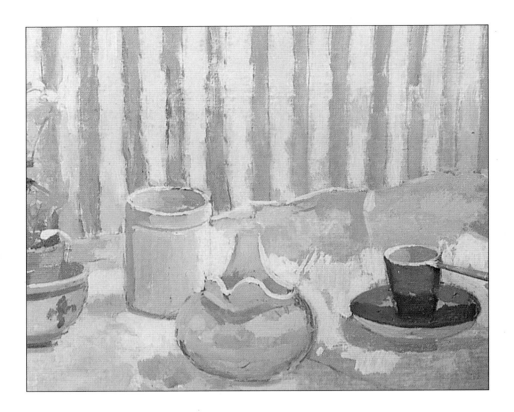

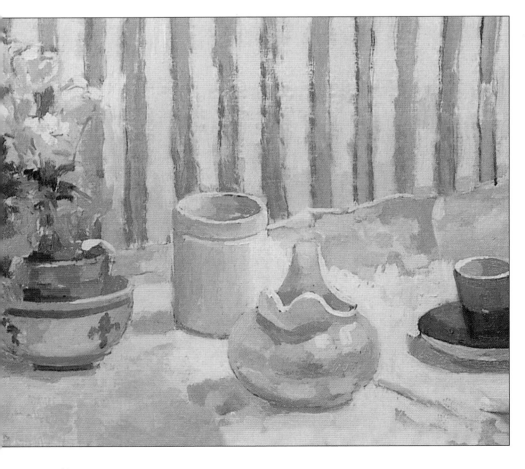

11 Squint up your eyes and look for the subtle changes in hue and tone in the glazed surface of the jug, which picks up and reflects colour from its surroundings. Use the no. 4 sable brush to touch in patches of colour – pale mauves, blues and pinks, greenish greys and bluish greys - using all the colours previously mixed on your palette. Then finish off the white cloth, using pure white for the lightest areas, modifying it with blues and greys from the palette for the shadows.

12 In this detail you can see how the artist has broken down the jug into separate 'patches' of colour. Each one is accurately observed in terms of shape, colour and tone, then its colour is mixed on the palette and applied decisively with brush strokes that follow the form of the jug. The separate tones are blended slightly, but not too much, thus retaining a lively paint quality. Note how the brightest highlights are modified with hints of Naples yellow and ultramarine so that they don't appear too stark.

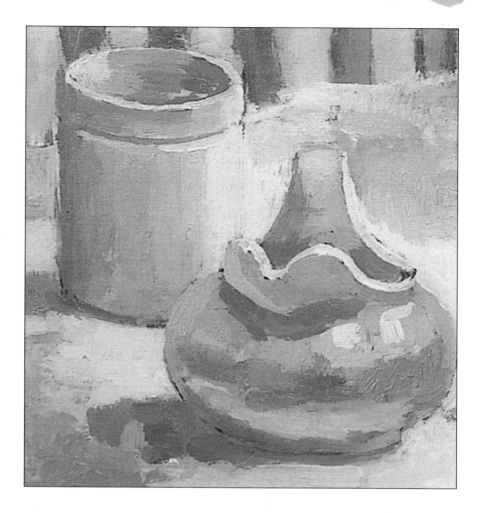

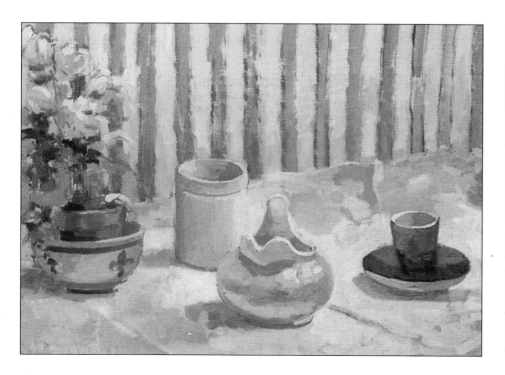

13 Continue making adjustments to the painting until you are satisfied with it, adding tiny touches of colour to modify the tones. Here, for example, the artist felt that the cyclamen flowers needed a little more definition, so he put in some dark pinks and strengthened the shapes of the petals. It is interesting to note the variety of colours that have been put into the whites in the painting – yet they still read as 'white'.

Painting Trees

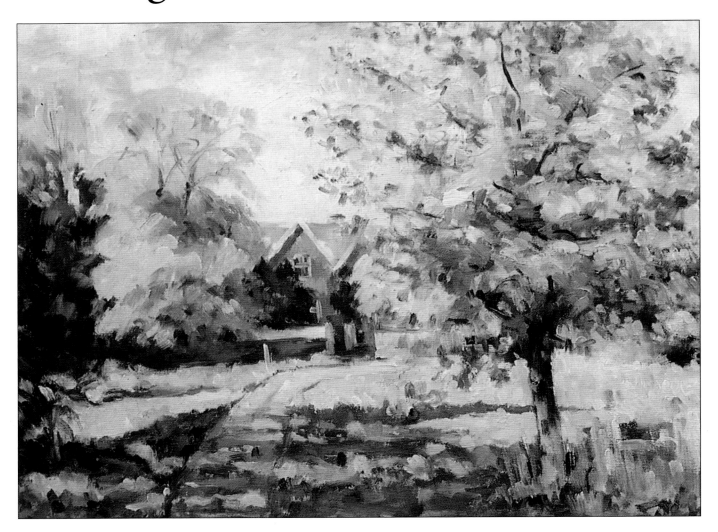

Ted Gould
AUTUMN TREES
Trees in their glorious autumn colours are captured expressively here with thick dabs and strokes of broken colour. Touches of blues and violets make the warm golds really 'sing'.

In a landscape, trees are usually seen from a distance; thus it is more important to capture their overall shape than to try to render every leaf and twig. Try to define the silhouette and 'gesture' of the particular tree species you are painting; an oak tree, for example, has a squat, rounded shape, while a poplar has a tall, distinctive, conical shape.

It is always necessary to simplify to some extent, whether you are painting bare winter trees or foliage-clad summer ones. Look for the large shapes and masses which characterize the tree and block these in broadly with thin paint, noting how each mass is modelled by light and shade. Then use thicker paint to develop the smaller branches and clumps of foliage. Finally, use descriptive brushwork to suggest some of the nearer foliage masses with more definition, and indicate one or two limbs and branches. The most important thing is to express the idea of the tree as a living, animate thing, so keep the edges of the foliage soft and feathery by merging them into the background wet-in-wet.

Proportions

A common mistake is misjudging the size of the leaf canopy in relation to the height of the trunk. Often it is painted too small, making the trees look like lollipops. Establish the correct proportions by comparing the width of the leaf canopy with its height from base to crown, then comparing the height of the visible trunk to the overall height of the tree.

Form and volume

Use light and shade to define the volume of trunks, branches and individual clumps of foliage; without attention to this aspect, your trees will appear flat and one-dimensional. Careful observation will show you that the light side of the tree will pick up warm colours, whereas the shadow side will contain hints of blue and violet reflected from the sky. Note also that not all the branches grow sideways; some will extend towards and away from you.

Sky holes

A tree is seldom, if ever, a solid mass of green. Even when a tree is in full foliage, there are always little light patches where the sky shows through, particularly around the outer edges of the branches. These 'sky holes' can be painted in last, which gives you a chance to redefine the shapes of the clumps of foliage.

Foliage colours

Try to see how many different colours you can find in the trees around you. Green is often the dominant colour, but the particular hue of green depends on the specific tree as well as on the season, the weather and the time of day. The foliage and branches of trees in spring often contain light greens, greys and even pinks. The full trees of summer contain rich, saturated greens, browns and rusts.

David Curtis
SLEET AND SNOW
Trees devoid of their summer foliage make dramatic shapes against a wintry sky. Here the thin, delicate twigs and branches are suggested with feathery drybrush strokes, working the outlines into the sky area to soften them.

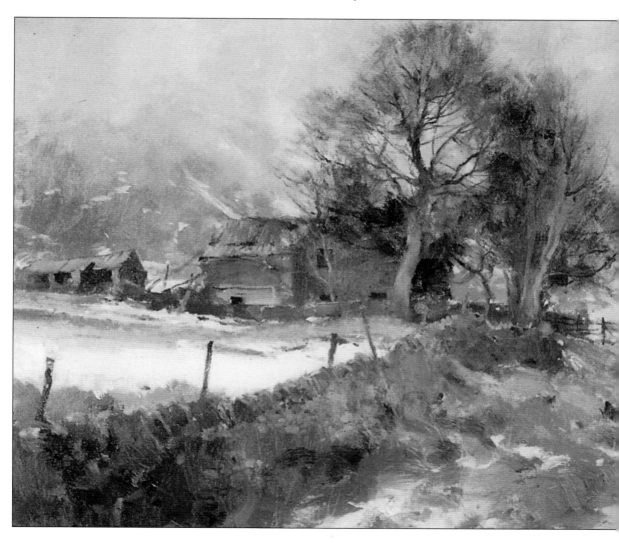

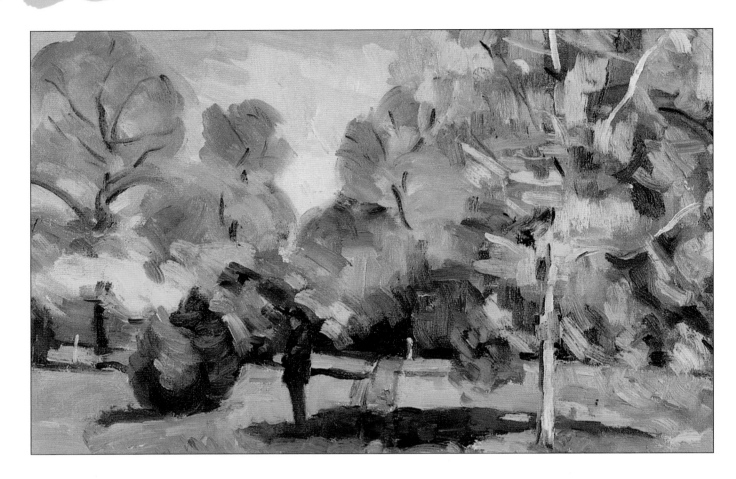

Autumn Trees

Landscapes and trees are favourite subjects for all oil painters, especially beginners. In this project we show you how to capture the essential characteristics of trees, their forms and textures, by using a variety of brush techniques to lend vitality and movement to your painting. Use bold, broad strokes to develop the trunk and branches, and descriptive brushwork for the foliage.

YOU WILL NEED

- ✓ Canvas board, 16 x 12in (40.6 x 30.5cm)
- ✓ No. 2 round bristle brush
- ✓ No. 5 flat bristle brush
- ✓ No. 4 long flat bristle brush
- ✓ Charcoal
- ✓ Rag
- ✓ Distilled turpentine
- ✓ Purified linseed oil

OIL PAINTS IN THE FOLLOWING COLOURS

- Spectrum yellow
- Yellow ochre
- Indian yellow
- Chrome orange
- Cobalt violet
- French ultramarine
- Manganese blue
- Chrome green
- Titanium white
- Mauve

1 Lightly sketch in the main outlines of the trees with a thin stick of charcoal. Use a clean cloth to gently flick off any excess charcoal dust so that it doesn't mix with the oil colours and dirty them.

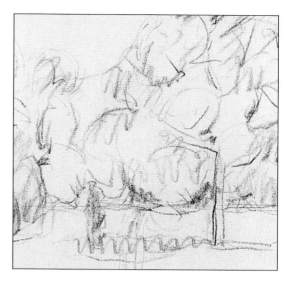

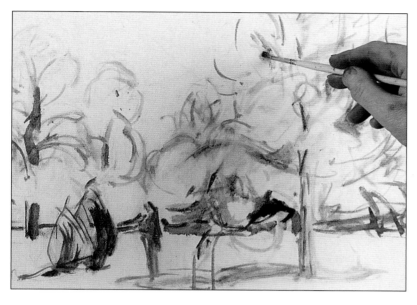

2 Using a no. 2 round bristle brush, mark in the main areas of the painting with mixtures of cobalt violet, French ultramarine, chrome green and yellow ochre. Dilute the paint with turpentine to a thin consistency and scrub it into the weave of the canvas. Add the outline of the figure in the foreground.

3 Block in the sky using a no. 5 flat bristle brush and a varied mix of white, manganese blue and French ultramarine diluted with turpentine. As you paint, use your colours only partially blended to add texture to the sky. Darken the mix with more ultramarine and a little yellow ochre and indicate the trees in the distance. Note how the artist has used vigorous, diagonal brush strokes which suggest the movement of the trees in the breeze (see detail above).

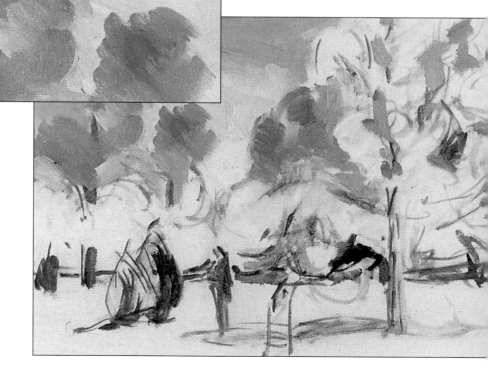

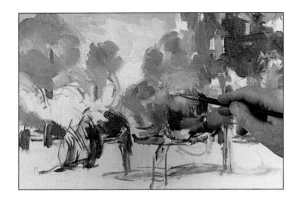

4 Mix a warm brown from cobalt violet and Indian yellow and block in the main clumps of foliage on the righthand tree. Twist and turn your brush to make both vertical and horizontal strokes. Dilute the paint with about 40% linseed oil and 60% turpentine. This makes the paint richer and easier to work with.

Helpful Hint
DON'T HOLD THE BRUSH TOO
CLOSE TO THE METAL FERRULE AS
THIS RESTRICTS MOVEMENT. HOLD
IT WHERE IT FEELS NATURALLY
BALANCED SO THAT YOUR BRUSH
MARKS WILL BE CONTROLLED
YET CONFIDENT.

5 Mix yellow ochre and Indian yellow for the autumn foliage on the trees. Add in a little chrome orange, chrome green and spectrum yellow. Work across the painting using varied combinations of green, yellow and orange, gradually filling in all the areas of foliage.

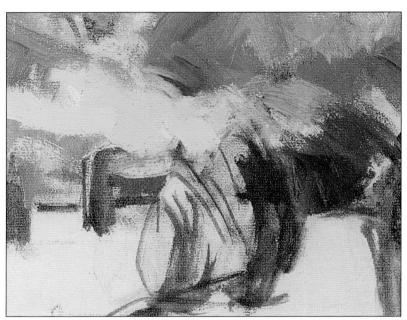

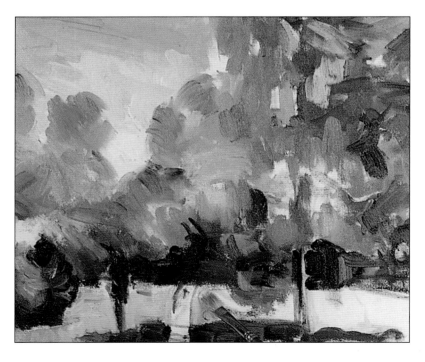

6 Now start painting the foreground using a no. 4 long flat bristle brush. Mix cobalt violet, ultramarine and chrome green to paint the darker, shadowy areas around the base of the trees and on the tree trunks. Mix a lighter green from ultramarine and chrome green for the light-struck foliage near the tops of the trees. Paint the fir trees in the foreground with the darker mix, adding some white to give the effect of light on the trees. Mix spectrum yellow with chrome green and yellow ochre for the grass, varying the proportions of each colour to add variety of tone and texture.

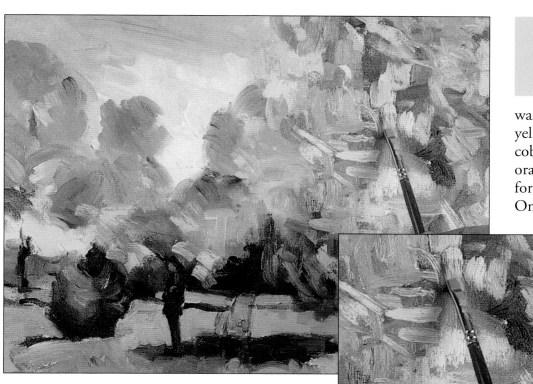

7 For the track in the centre of the picture mix a warm brown from Indian yellow, chrome orange and cobalt violet. Mix yellows, orange and a little violet for the autumn leaves. Once again vary the tones and move the brush vertically and horizontally across the canvas to build up an energetic paint surface (see detail left).

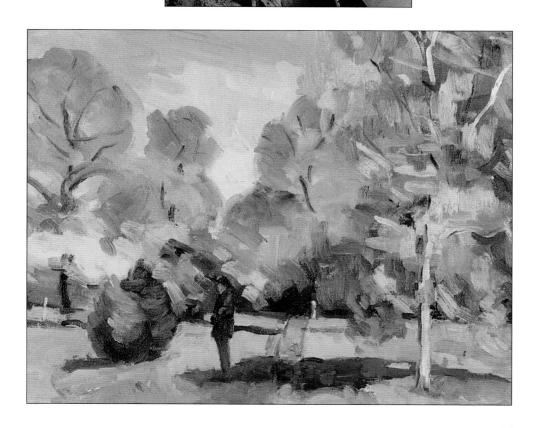

8 Paint the right–hand tree trunk and branches with titanium white, letting the colour underneath break into it. Using the no. 2 round bristle brush, now add the dark trunk and branches using a mixture of ultramarine and mauve. Define the figure in the foreground with the same mixture. Finally, move around the picture adding touches of colour to introduce more detail and texture.

Painting Flowers and Leaves

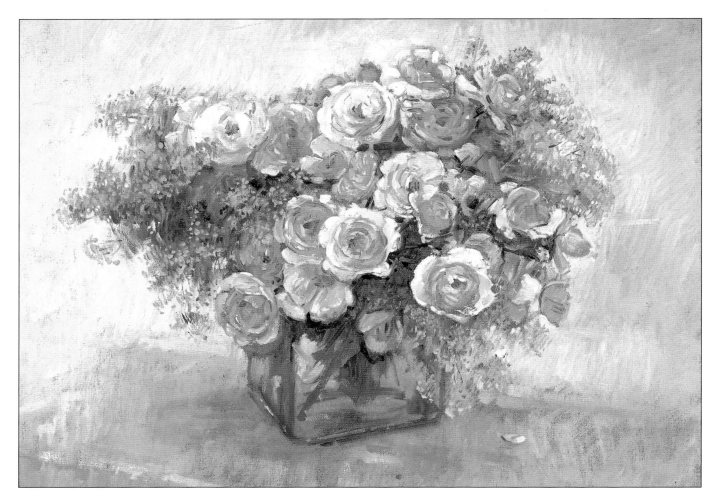

From tiny meadow flowers growing in the wild to hot-house exotics such as orchids, flowers and leaves are an infinitely appealing subject to paint. The approaches to painting them are equally varied. If it's the subtle coloration of the blooms and foliage that appeals to you, or a particular species of flower, you might choose to concentrate on a single leaf or flower – or even to close in on one or two petals so that your work becomes semi-abstract. Bouquets of cut flowers allow you to explore a number of different blooms in the same arrangement. Alternatively, you might want to paint a floral landscape – a field full of poppies or lavender, perhaps.

Whatever approach you take and whatever medium you are working in, start with the overall shape. Make studies in your sketchbook, looking at how the petals

Philip Miller
ALCHEMILLA AND ROSES
This lovely oil study effectively contrasts both colour and shape, the delicate and "frothy" stems of bright, yellowy green alchemilla providing a lovely foil to the more rounded forms of the roses.

and leaves overlap, where the flower head sits in relation to the stalk, the size and shape of the leaves and so on. The better you understand the structure, the better your painting will be.

Colour is undoubtedly one of the main reasons for painting flowers; the rich golds and russets of autumn leaves are stunning. If you are painting in oils or acrylics, thin glazes are a good way of conveying the delicacy of petals and leaves; the colours mix optically on the support, creating subtle blends that would be difficult, to achieve in the palette. The equivalent technique in gouache is to work thinly in semi-transparent washes, allowing each wash to modify the wash beneath.

Working wet into wet in any medium will enable you to convey subtle shifts of tone. In gouache and thin acrylics, you can allow the colours to flow and merge on the support of their own accord; although the technique is somewhat unpredictable, with practice you will have more control. In thicker acrylics and in oils, working wet into wet allows the artist to blend the paint on the support, feathering brushstrokes to create subtle transitions in tone.

Textures are important too. Exploit the full range of textural techniques – drybrush work for linear details on petals or leaves, scumbling one colour over another, dabbing paint on thickly with a painting knife to convey a mass of small flowers.

If you're painting several flowers together, choose a viewpoint that allows you to see some of them from the side, rather than straight on. This makes it easier to see the structure of the bloom and make it look three-dimensional.

LOVAGE, CLEMATIS AND SHADOWS
In this scene, it is the shadows cast by the stems, rather than the flowers that caught the artist's eye. They bring the painting to life.

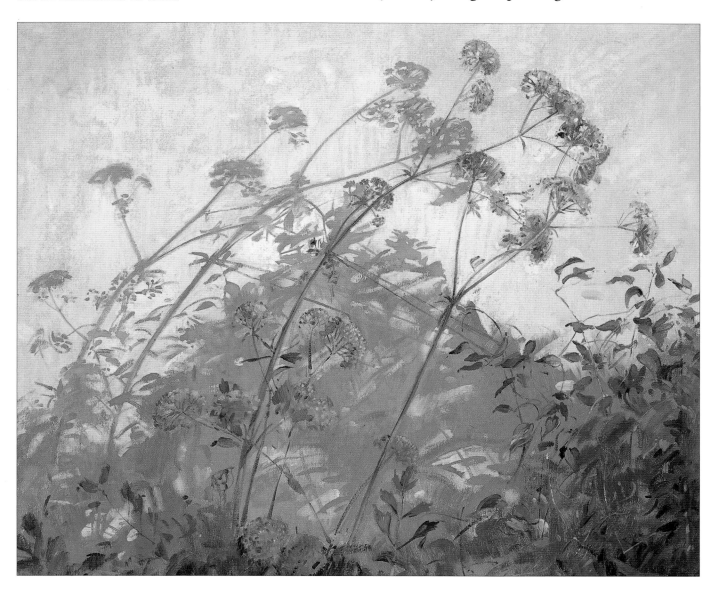

Tulips in a Vase

In this simple still life, a bunch of pink and green parrot tulips has been placed in a turquoise glass vase that complements their shape beautifully. When you paint a subject like this, with overlapping shapes and twisting stems, look at the spaces between as well as at the flowers and stems.

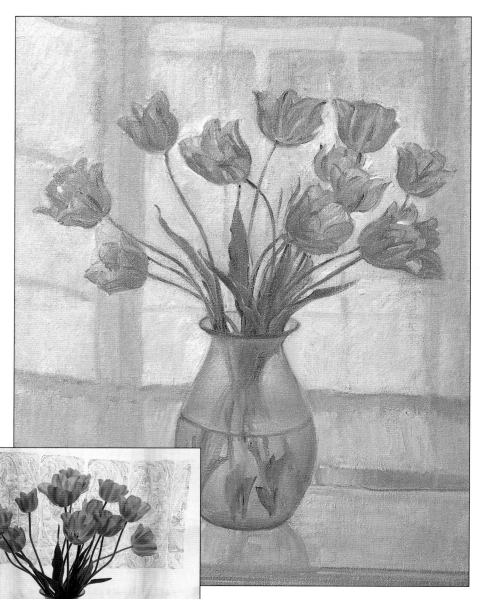

YOU WILL NEED

☐ Primed canvas board, 14 x 9¹/₂in (35.6 x 24.2cm)
☐ No. 2 round sable brush
☐ No. 5 round bristle brush
☐ 1¹/₂in (38mm) decorating brush
☐ Distilled turpentine
☐ Refined linseed oil
☐ Dammar varnish

OIL PAINTS IN THE FOLLOWING COLOURS

- Olive green
- Raw sienna
- Viridian
- Yellow ochre
- Indian yellow
- Lemon yellow
- Titanium white

- Madder lake
- Caesar purple
- Cadmium red
- Cobalt blue
- Cerulean blue
- Phthalocyanine turquoise

1 Mix a dull brown from olive green and raw sienna. Using a small brush, draw the overall lines and shapes of the flowers and vase. Put in the glazing bars, which can be seen through the curtain, and the window ledge.

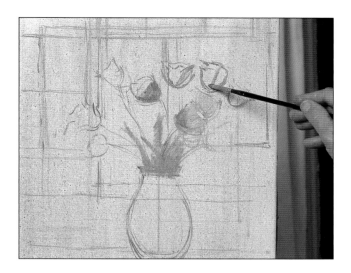

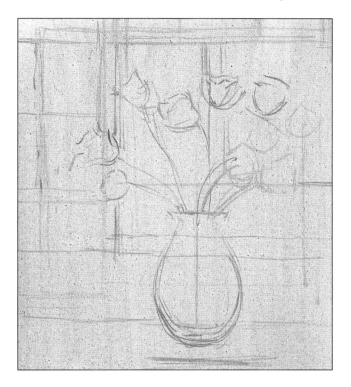

2 Mix greens for the leaves and stalks (viridian, yellow ochre and Indian yellow for the warmer dark and mid-toned areas, and viridian, lemon yellow, and titanium white for the more acidic areas). Mix pinks for the flowers (madder lake and white, with a touch of blue for the cooler shades, and Caesar purple and white). Vary the proportions of the colours to give a good range of tones. Using a mid-toned and a slightly bluer green, put in the stalks and leaves protruding from the vase. Start to block in the flowers.

Helpful Hint

PUT DOWN GUIDELINES, SUCH AS A VERTICAL LINE THROUGH THE CENTRE OF THE VASE. TURN YOUR PAINTING UPSIDE DOWN TO CHECK THE SHAPES. THIS MAKES IT EASIER TO SEE OBJECTS AS GEOMETRIC FORMS.

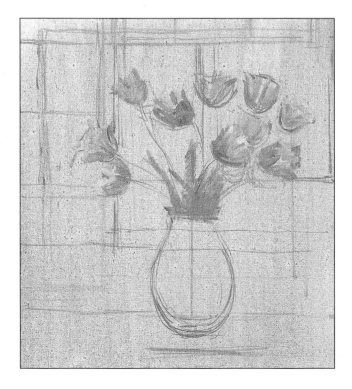

3 Continue to block in the flowers, adjusting the proportions of the colours in your mixes to get the right tone. Because of their position in relation to the light, some flowers are much warmer in tone than others: add a little cadmium red for these mixes. In others, where petals overlap, a deeper shade of purple can be seen. Work methodically: you need to assess tones and colours continually as you work.

4 Using various dark greens, paint the stalks. Mix a bright blue from cobalt blue and titanium white and put in the darkest areas at the top of the vase, and the water line halfway up. Mix cerulean blue and white for the light blues in the top half of the vase, and a greener blue for the water.

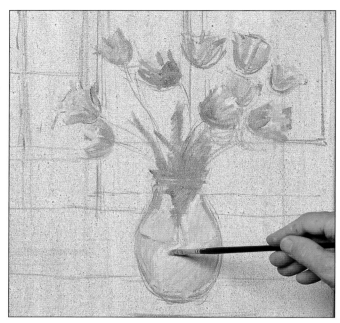

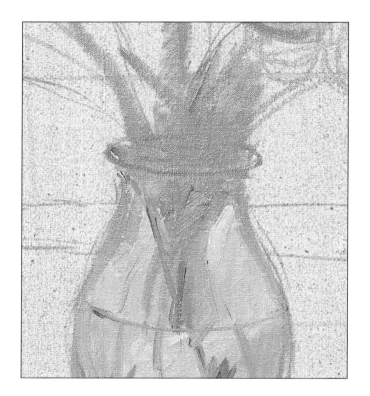

5 Paint the stems that are underwater, using a darker green. The shapes are slightly distorted by being seen through water; the colours are also softened by the opaque glass of the vase. You can create these effects by blending the green into the underlying wet paint.

6 Mix a pale, creamy brown colour by adding Indian yellow and white to the bright green that you used you used on the flower heads. Begin blocking in the dark panel in the centre of the muslin curtain behind the flowers, taking care not to obliterate the lines of the glazing bars completely. Outside the central panel, the curtain is lighter in tone. Mix blue and white and scumble the colour on loosely, allowing some of the toned ground to show through to create the texture of the woven fabric. Paint more of the stems, noting how they twist and turn over one another.

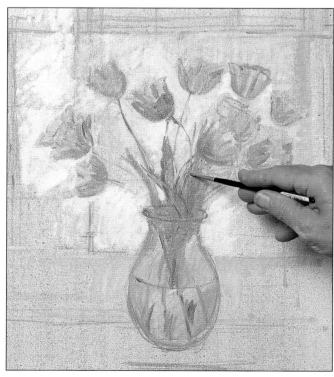

7 Using the tip of a small sable brush, sharpen the edges of the flowers to give them a crisp outline, and put in some linear detail on the petals, using a deep purplish pink and a bright, acidic green as appropriate. You can see that the flowers almost immediately begin to take on more of a sense of form and to stand out more clearly from the neutral-coloured background; they are no longer merely flat blocks of colour.

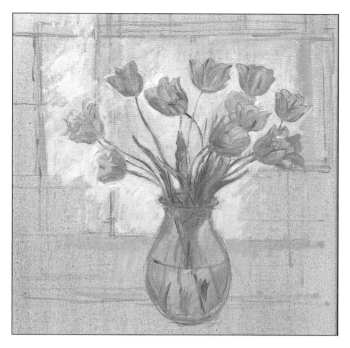

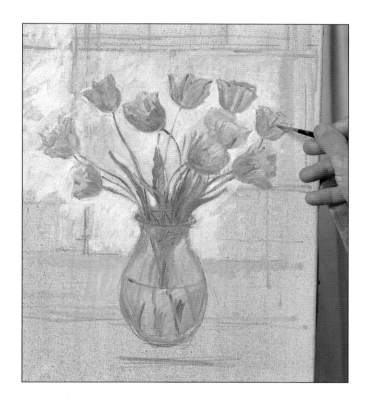

8 Continue to refine the details, working on the tonal changes within the petals to create some sense of depth and form. As before, half-close your eyes as you look at the scene, to see where the changes in tone occur.

9 Paint the deep hem of the curtain in the same mixture that you used for the central panel. The darker colour means that the flowers have something to register against. Don't obscure the glazing bars since they will be reinforced later.

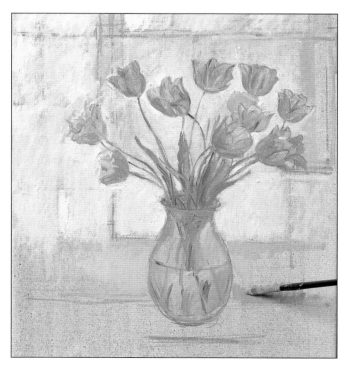

61

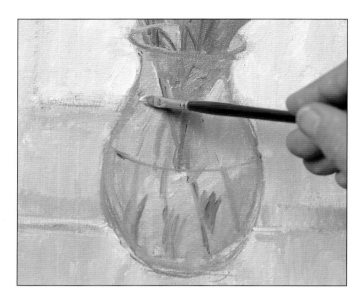

10 The vase is reflected in the window ledge. Put in this reflection, using slightly curved brushstrokes that echo the form of the vase, and leaving some gaps to create the effect of shimmering light. Work more pale blue into the vase interior, carefully painting around the flower stems.

11 Using the same neutral background colours as before, work around the vase, sharpening the edges and softening any areas that are overly blue. Using a pale, neutral blue-grey, strengthen the glazing bars that can be seen through the fabric. Strengthen the greens of the stems in the water. Look at the negative spaces between the stems as well as at the stems themselves. Reinforce the shadow cast by the vase on the window ledge.

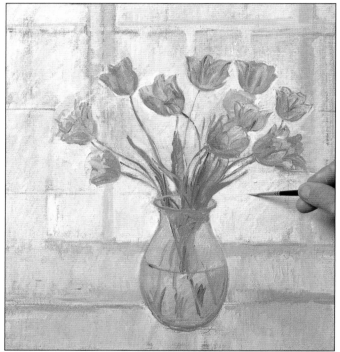

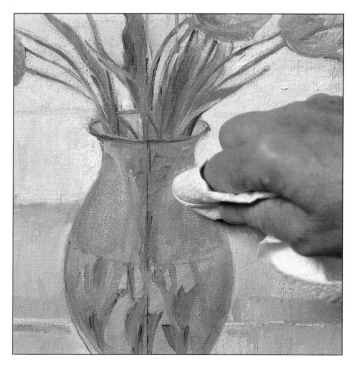

12 At this point, the artist realized that the shape of the glass vase was not quite right. He also felt that the blue he had used for the vase was not vibrant enough. Because the paint was still wet, he was able to scrape it off with a knife and repaint, using a mixture of phthalocyanine turquoise and white. He then wiped off some of the turquoise paint with a piece of absorbent paper to soften the colour and create the effect of light being diffused through the glass.

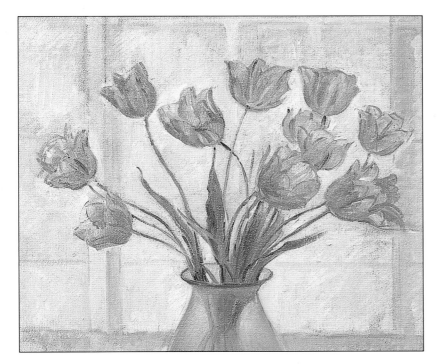

13 Gently stroke a paler version of the phthalocyanine turquoise and titanium white mixture used in Step 15 over the top half of the vase, blending the colours wet into wet, to heighten the effect of soft, diffused light coming through the glass.

Helpful Hint
THE MORE CAREFULLY TOO LOOK AT PLANTS, THE BETTER YOUR PAINTINGS WILL BE. MAKE QUICK SKETCHES WHENEVER YOU CAN.

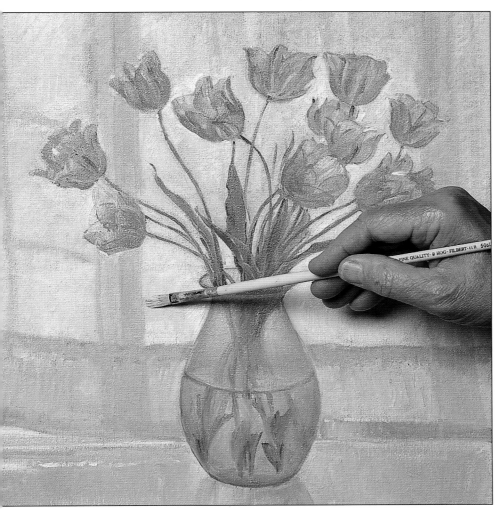

14 In the final stages, the lighting changed. Mix a range of greys from cobalt blue, white and a little Caesar purple and put in the shadows cast by the glazing bars. Warm up the neutral background mixture by adding Indian yellow, and scumble it over the background.

Underpainting

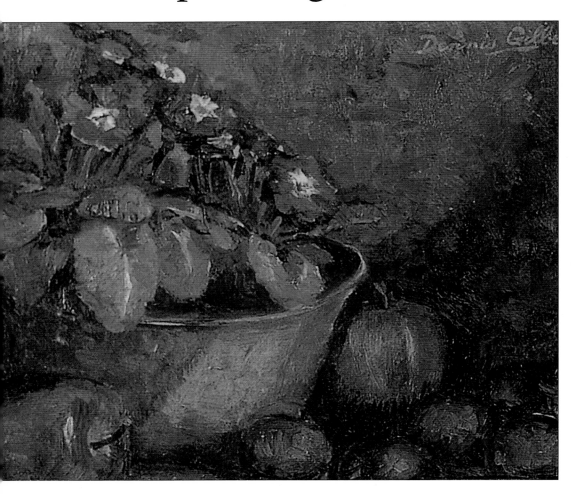

**Dennis Gilbert
RED STILL LIFE**
When tackling an intricate subject like this one, starting with an underpainting can help by providing a tonal 'blueprint' of the final image. Knowing that the composition and tonal values are sound, you can proceed with confidence and thus retain the freshness of your first impression.

The traditional way of starting an oil painting is to block in the main shapes, masses and tones of the composition with thin paint in a neutral colour, before adding the main details and surface colours and textures. The basic principle is to give you an idea of what the final image will look like before you begin the painting proper.

Composition, drawing, proportion, the distribution of light and shade – all of these elements can be checked, and any alterations made quite easily at this stage. Because the paint used for underpainting is so thin, any alterations needed can be easily effected by wiping the paint with a rag soaked in turpentine; this will not be possible in the subsequent stages, as you run the risk of overworking the painting and spoiling the colour mix.

The result is a practical division of labour; once the underpainting is complete you can begin working in colour, confident that the composition and tonal values are sound. This is the time-honoured method of painting in oils, used by Rembrandt, Rubens and many other great masters.

When underpainting in oils, always keep in mind the principle of working 'fat over lean': the paint should be thinly diluted with turpentine and allowed to dry thoroughly before adding further layers. To save time, fast-drying colours such as raw umber, cobalt blue and terre verte are the most convenient to use.

Alternatively, use acrylic paint for the underpainting. This dries within minutes, allowing you to begin the overpainting in oils in the same session.

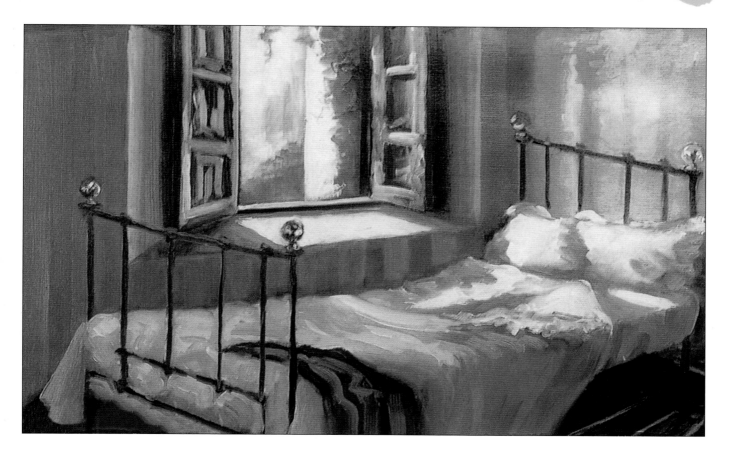

The Boudoir

It was important to assess the light and dark tones accurately in order to recreate the effect of vibrant light in this sunny interior. By starting with an underpainting, the artist was able to control the tonal balance of the image from the beginning, without being distracted by colour. Tones of blue-grey were used for the underpainting, to harmonize with the cool, shadowy tones of the bedroom.

OIL PAINTS IN THE FOLLOWING COLOURS

- *Monestial turquoise*
- *Monestial blue*
- *French ultramarine*
- *Indigo*
- *Winsor violet*
- *Burnt sienna*
- *Brown ochre*
- *Yellow ochre*
- *Lemon yellow*
- *Rowney red*

YOU WILL NEED

- *Sheet of primed canvas or board, 16¹/₂ x 12in (41.9 x 30.5cm)*
- *³/₄in (19mm) flat synthetic fibre brush*
- *No. 4 flat synthetic fibre brush*
- *No. 6 flat synthetic fibre brush*
- *HB pencil*
- *Distilled turpentine*
- *Small piece of muslin*
- *Kitchen paper*

1 When painting a complex subject, it's a good idea to make a pencil sketch of it first. Refer to the sketch as you paint, using it to check the perspective lines and the arrangement of light and dark tones. Drawing a grid over the sketch (use tracing paper if you prefer) makes it easier to transfer the composition to your canvas; draw a grid in the same proportions on the canvas, then transfer the image that appears in each square on the sketch to its equivalent square on the canvas.

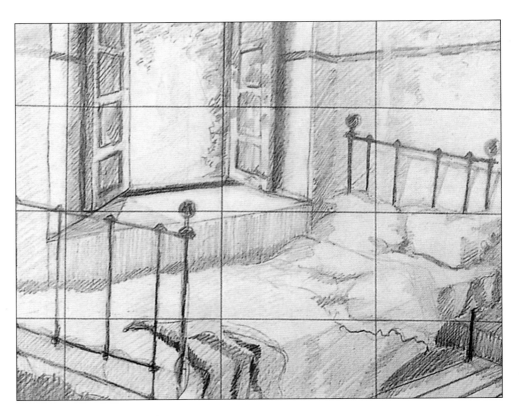

2 Mix a wash of monestial turquoise, thinly diluted with turpentine, and apply this over the entire board with the ³/₄in (19mm) flat brush. This eliminates the stark whiteness of the primed canvas board. Add a touch of indigo to the mixture and block in the dark tones – the window frame, the picture rail and the shadows around the bed. Now wrap a piece of muslin round your finger, dip it in turpentine and rub into the wet colour, back to the white priming, to introduce the light tones on the window and the bed.

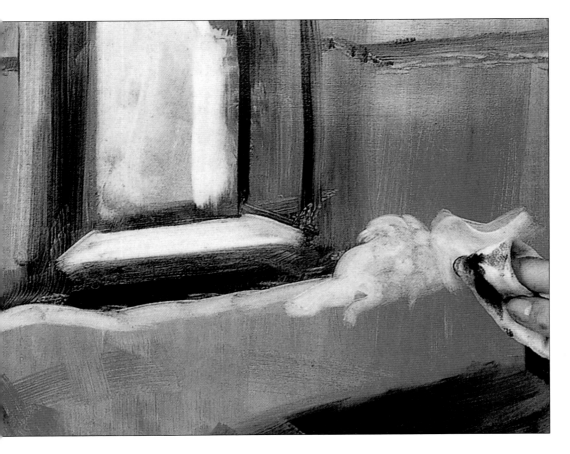

3 Here we see how the artist has described the rumpled sheets and pillows by 'drawing' into the wet paint with the muslin. The tone of the wall on the right has also been lightened. Now, using the chisel edge of the no. 4 flat brush and the monestial turquoise and indigo mixture, put in the lines on the window shutters and paint the metal bedstead.

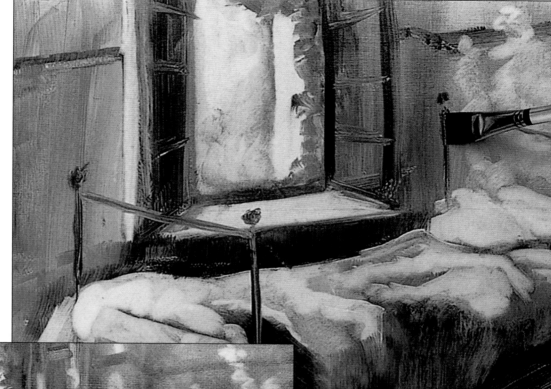

Helpful Hint
AS YOU WORK, KEEP CHECKING ONE DARK AREA AGAINST ANOTHER TO SEE WHETHER OR NOT THE TONES ARE SIMILAR, THEN CHECK THEM AGAINST THE LIGHTER AREAS. OVER-ESTIMATING THE DIFFERENCES BETWEEN TONES CREATES A CONFUSED, 'JUMPY' IMAGE. ALWAYS KEEP AN EYE ON THE WHOLE IMAGE AS WELL AS INDIVIDUAL PARTS.

4 Build up an informative under-painting, adding the details on the shutters and bedstead with broad brushstrokes. Start to refine the broad shapes of light and dark on the bed linen and the dressing gown draped over the foot of the bed. Add a little more indigo to the mix and loosely describe the foliage glimpsed through the window. Suggest the frilled edges of the sheets and pillows by working into the wet paint once more with the damp muslin, pushing your fingernail through to the cloth to describe the intricate curves.

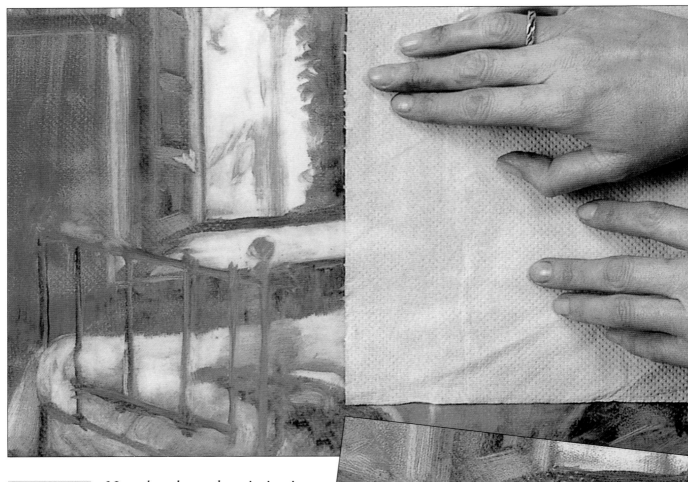

5 Now that the underpainting is completed you can start to build up the details. To create a surface with more 'grip' for the further application of paint, try the following technique: lay a sheet of absorbent paper such as kitchen paper over the painting and gently smooth it down using a circular movement. Then peel away the paper to remove any excess oily paint, creating a more sympathetic surface to work on. Leave the painting to dry for approximately 24 hours. This method is known as 'tonking' (after a former professor of painting named Henry Tonks). In the detail (right) you can see how the tonking method creates a pleasing, softly textured surface. The main structure of the painting is firmly established, but the colours are softened and lightened, making it easier to continue adding more detail on top.

6 Now start to introduce the warm tones in the room. Partially mix titanium white, Winsor purple and brown ochre. Using a no. 4 flat brush, sketch in the view through the window with loose, fluid brushstrokes, working the colours wet into wet. Use pure white on the sunlit wall. Add warm highlights on the sunlit leaves with white and a little yellow ochre. For the shadowy leaves use monestial turquoise and monestial blue. Paint the wooden shutters with a thin wash of burnt sienna. Touch in the knobs on the bedstead with brown ochre.

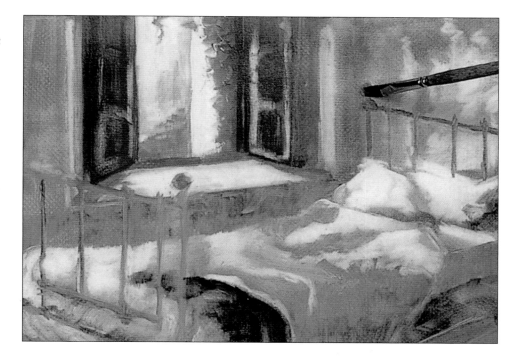

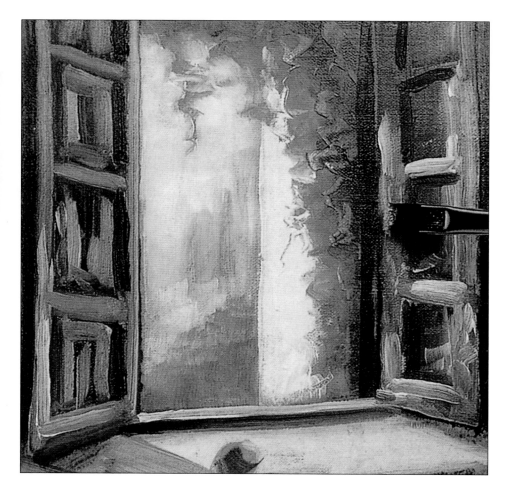

7 To make the view through the window appear to recede, concentrate stronger detail and colour on the window itself to bring it forward. Block in the shutters with a mix of raw umber and indigo. Then mix yellow ochre, burnt sienna and white and define the carved detailing on the shutters. Where warm light strikes the edges of the shutters, use a warm orange mixed from Rowney red, yellow ochre and lemon yellow. For the cooler glints of light, add touches of white and lemon yellow. Paint the shadows cast by the shutters on the windowsill with monestial turquoise and indigo.

8 Sunlight streaming in through the open window gives the shadows on the walls a luminous blue-violet tint. Use a no. 6 flat brush to paint the walls with monestial turquoise and white, working in some Winsor violet and white for the shadow areas. For the shadow on the wall beneath the window, mix indigo and Winsor violet. Paint the window alcove with a mix of monestial blue, white and a touch of ultramarine. Sketch in the picture rail with a mix of indigo and burnt umber and define the edge of the window alcove with white and lemon yellow.

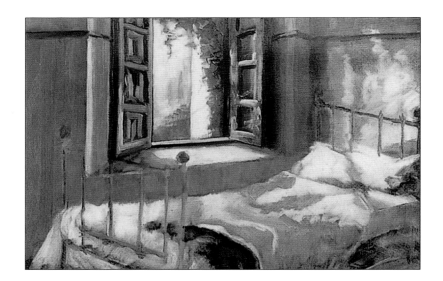

9 Soften the colour of the wall on the right with a mix of ultramarine and white. Work into the shadows under the bed with indigo and a little raw umber, then scratch lines into the wet paint with the end of the brush handle to suggest the floorboards. With the no. 4 brush, define the metal bedstead with indigo. Mix lemon yellow with just a touch of Rowney red and dot in the bright highlights on the shiny brass bed knobs.

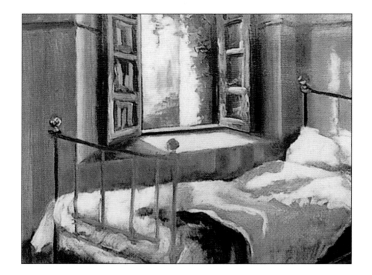

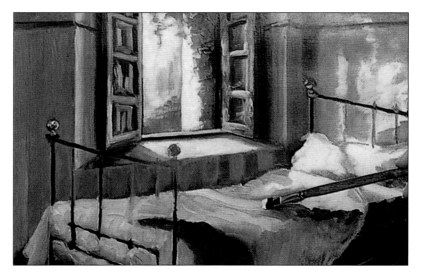

10 Now start to define the cool shadows and warm lights on the white bed linen. Go over the shadows established in the underpainting with shades of ultramarine and monestial blue. Where the sheet folds over the end of the bed the shadows have a more violet cast – paint these with a mix of Winsor violet and white. Then mix white and yellow ochre to pick up the highlights on the pillows and sheets.

11 Suggest the striped pattern of the dressing gown with Rowney red and a mix of monestial blue and white. Finish defining the bedstead with indigo and complete the brass knobs with raw umber for the shadows, a little Rowney red for the reflections and lemon yellow for the bright highlights. Deepen the shadow on the sheet falling over the edge of the bed with a mixture of ultramarine, Winsor violet and white. Mix white with just a hint of ultramarine and begin painting the brighter whites where light from the window is shining directly on to the bed.

Helpful Hint
WHITE OBJECTS REFLECT COLOUR FROM THEIR SURROUNDINGS, SO THEY RARELY APPEAR PURE WHITE BUT A COMPOSITE OF MANY COLOURS. IN THIS SUNNY ROOM THE WHITE BED LINEN CONTAINS COOL BLUES AND VIOLETS IN THE SHADOWS AND WARM CREAMS AND YELLOWS IN THE HIGHLIGHTS.

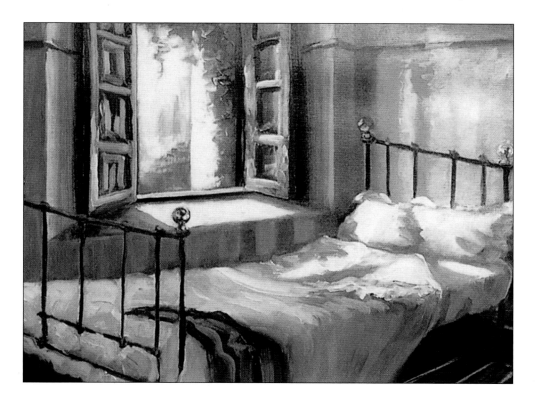

12 Use the same mixture to paint the pillows and suggest their frilled edges, and to soften and blend the shadows and highlights on the righthand wall. Finally, use touches of pure white to accentuate the dappled light that falls across the windowsill and over the bed.

Developing the Painting

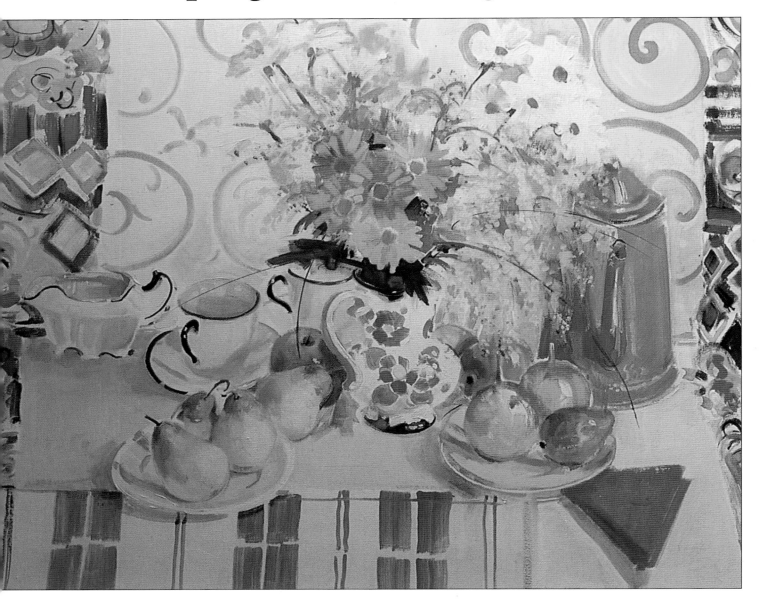

Peter Graham
LE PETIT DÉJEUNER
**This artist always starts his paintings with washes
of thin colour, well diluted with turpentine,
to indicate the broad forms of the composition.
By building up the colours gradually, he keeps
the final painting fresh and lively.**

A mistake sometimes made by inexperienced
painters is to work on one small area of a painting
until it is 'finished', and then move on to the next
area. However, this can result in a confused and
disjointed image because each area of tone and
colour is separate and unrelated to its neighbours.

Instead of working in this piecemeal fashion, try
to work over all areas of the canvas at the same
time, moving from foreground to background and
letting the composition weave itself into a whole.
The image should emerge gradually, similar to the
way a photographic image comes into focus in
the developing tray.

Balancing colours

Keep your eyes moving around the subject, looking for the way tones, colours and shapes relate to each other and making adjustments as you go. You need to do this because the tones and colours you apply to your canvas do not work in isolation – they are influenced by the tones and colours surrounding them. For example, a tone which appears dark on its own will suddenly appear much lighter when surrounded by darker tones. Similarly, a warm colour may appear quite cool when surrounded by even warmer colours. Painting is a continuous process of balancing, judging, altering and refining – which is what makes it so absorbing.

Building up

If you apply too many heavy layers of paint in the early stages, you may find that the surface quickly becomes clogged and the paint eventually builds up to a slippery, churned-up mess. To avoid this you need to pace yourself in the early stages – it is a mistake to try to get to the finished picture too soon.

When you start a painting, bear in mind the advice of Cézanne: "start with the broom and end with the needle!" In other words, work from the general to the particular. Start by rapidly laying in the broad shapes and colour masses of the composition with thin colour before starting to develop the detail.

Dennis Gilbert
WASHING LINE, MURANO
The harmony and unity of this picture was achieved by working over the whole painting at once, so that colour was picked up on the brush and transferred to other areas, thus allowing the image to emerge gradually from the canvas.

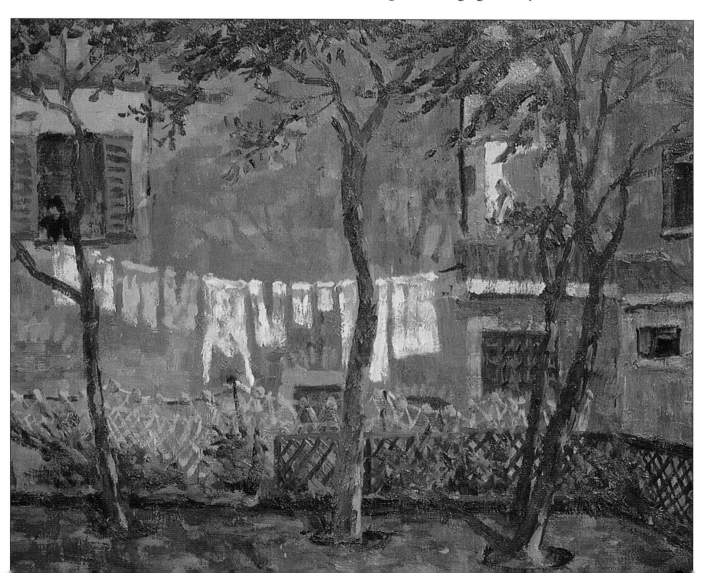

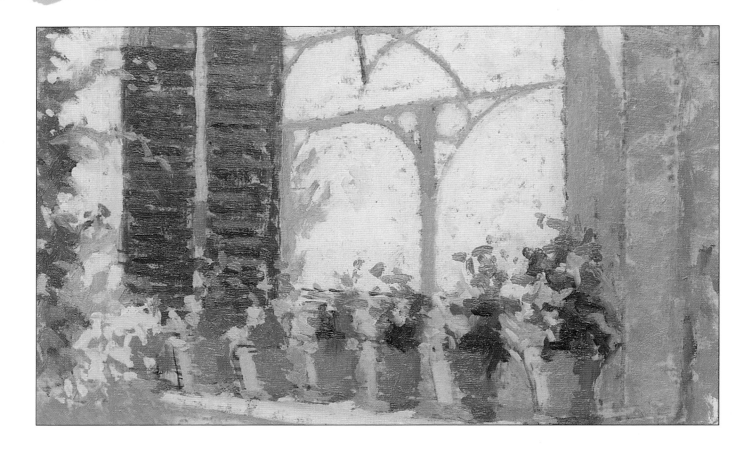

Terrace in Tuscany

A successful composition weaves itself into a whole. To capture the unifying effect of bright sunlight on this scene, the artist worked over the whole painting at once, so that paint was picked up on the brush and transferred to other areas of the canvas.

OIL PAINTS IN THE FOLLOWING COLOURS

- *Raw umber*
- *Raw sienna*
- *Burnt sienna*
- *Cadmium orange*
- *Yellow ochre*
- *Chrome green*
- *Cadmium red*
- *Alizarin crimson*

- *Titanium white*
- *French ultramarine*
- *Ivory black*
- *Veridian*
- *Lemon yellow*
- *Cobalt blue*
- *Vermilion*

YOU WILL NEED

- ☐ *Sheet of primed board, 20 x 16in (50.8 x 40.6cm)*
- ☐ *No. 3 round sable bristle brush*
- ☐ *No. 4 round bristle brush*
- ☐ *No. 6 round bristle brush*
- ☐ *Distilled turpentine*
- ☐ *Purified linseed oil*
- ☐ *Dammar varnish*

1 Prepare your board in advance by tinting it with a warm brown mixed from raw umber and raw sienna. Dilute the paint with plenty of turpentine and apply it loosely with a 1in (25mm) decorating brush. Leave to dry for 24 hours. Using a no. 3 round sable brush, draw the main outlines of the composition with thinly diluted burnt sienna.

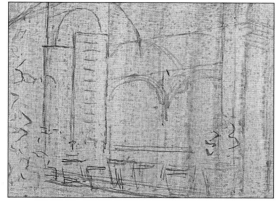

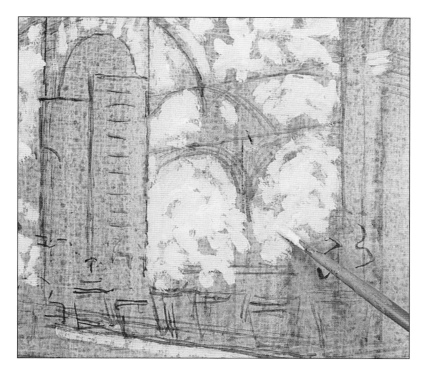

2 Start to block in the stone wall of the house with a light golden yellow mixed from varied combinations of cadmium orange, yellow ochre and titanium white. Mix the paint with a medium consisting of equal parts of linseed oil and dammar varnish plus twice the volume of turpentine. Apply the paint with a no. 6 round bristle brush using short brushstrokes worked in different directions. Allow some of the background wash to show through.

3 Paint the climbing plant on the left with a mixture of French ultramarine, chrome green and ivory black, varying the tones from light to dark. Suggest the slatted wooden shutters with a mixture of burnt sienna, alizarin crimson and a little cadmium red. To paint the part of the wall that falls in shadow on the right you will need chrome green, burnt sienna, alizarin crimson, cadmium red and French ultramarine. Mix the colours in varying combinations to create a variety of tones ranging from grey to a greenish brown.

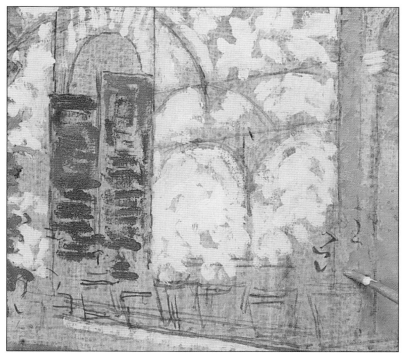

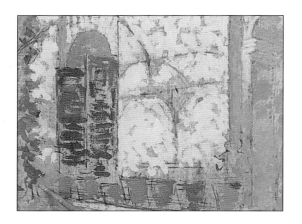

4 Mix burnt sienna, cadmium red, alizarin crimson and white to make a rich terracotta and use this to rough in the shadow sides of the plant pots. Paint the arch above the shutters with the same combination of colours used for the shadowy wall in step 3. Use the same mix to suggest the dappled shadows cast by the foliage on the bottom left of the picture.

5 Continue building up the picture loosely, keeping an eye on the overall effect. Resume work on the background wall and the shutters, using the same colours mixed earlier. Switch to a no. 4 round bristle brush and define the shadow cast by the pergola onto the wall with a purple-grey mixed from ultramarine and cadmium red. Work on the climber and the geranium leaves, adding a little yellow ochre to the original foliage colour used in step 3 for the warmer tones.

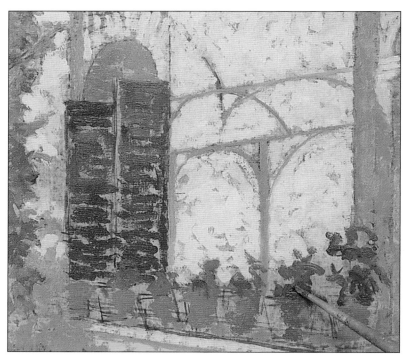

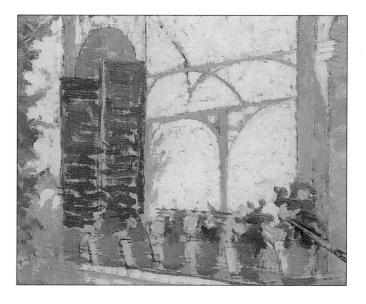

6 Continue building up the colour on the background wall. Add subtle hints of lighter tone to the shadow of the pergola by adding cobalt blue and a little white to the original mix. Use the same colour for the dappled shadows either side of the shutters. Mix viridian and ultramarine for the small trays under the plant pots. Put in the warm lights on the plant pots with touches of cadmium orange and a dusky pink mixed from alizarin, white and a touch of burnt sienna. Paint the sunlit geranium leaves using white, chrome green and lemon yellow.

7 Give more definition to the shutters, adding more alizarin to the original mix for the darker slats and a little white for the highlights. Define the sunlit edge of the shutter with a mix of cadmium orange, lemon yellow and white. Use the same colour to suggest the trailing plant in the lefthand corner. Mix lemon yellow, chrome green and white for the light-struck leaves on the climber. Use a no. 3 round sable brush to paint the green metal arch of the pergola with a mixture of viridian and ultramarine, lightened with white.

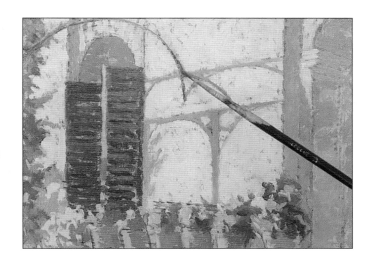

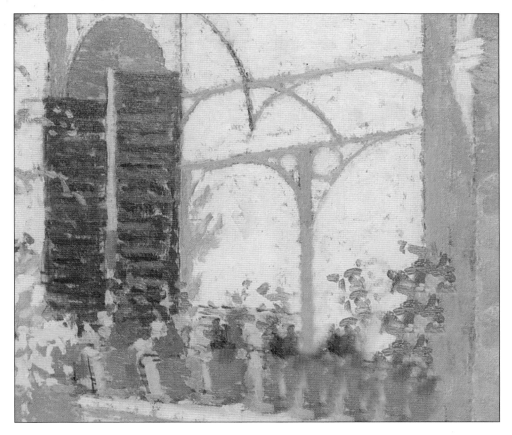

8 Bring some sprigs of foliage out across the shutter on the left to create a sense of three-dimensional space. Add touches of richer colour to the terracotta plant pots with mixes of burnt sienna, cadmium red and cadmium orange. Finally, paint the brilliant red geranium flowers with short strokes of vermilion, letting the brushstrokes themselves form the shapes of the petals. This detail (left) of the geraniums illustrates the way in which paint can be used to create texture. The flowers and leaves are suggested by short, curving brush-strokes, using thick paint over a still-wet layer beneath it so that each colour is modified by the one beneath.

Helpful Hint
AS YOUR PAINTING NEARS COMPLETION, TAKE A BREAK FROM IT SO THAT WHEN YOU COME BACK TO IT YOU CAN LOOK AT IT AFRESH.

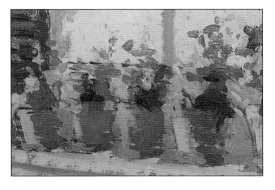

Colour Harmony

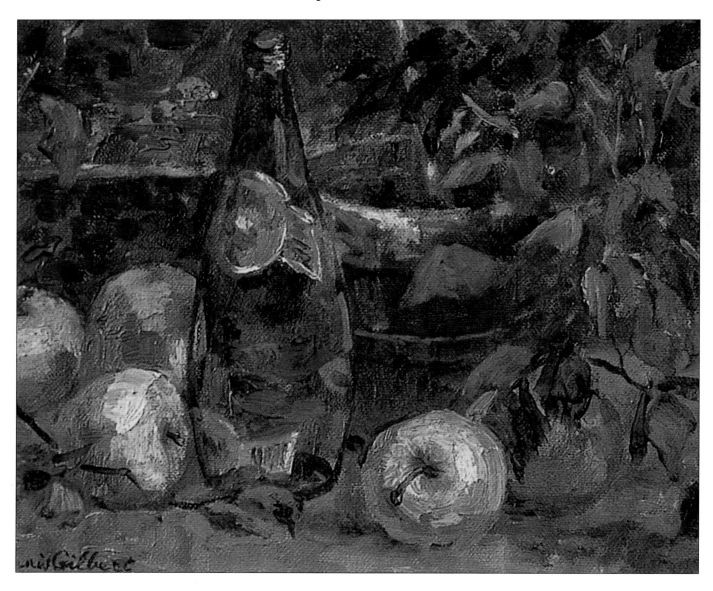

Dennis Gilbert
GREEN STILL LIFE
**The cool greens and yellows in this painting
are offset by smaller touches of warm earth
colours; creating an image that is harmonious
but not monotonous.**

Think of the tones and colours in a painting as
musical notes. It you include too many colour
'notes' in your picture it becomes confused and
'out of tune'. But if you use them in a controlled
range, you will produce an image that is not only
balanced and harmonious but also more powerful
and intense.

Analogous colours

An effective way of creating harmony in a painting
is to focus on a selection of colours which lie next
to each other on the colour wheel; these are called
analogous colours. They work together well since
they share a common base colour. Harmonious
colour schemes include be blue, blue-green and
blue-violet; or orange, red-orange and yellow-orange.

Nature provides ample inspiration for harmonious colour schemes. Think of the golds, russets and reds of an autumn landscape, the subtle shades of blue and green in a river or sea, or the pinks, violets and indigos of the sky at twilight.

There is a risk, of course, that too much harmony can make a rather bland, insipid painting. One way to avoid this is to include a small area of contrasting colour in the composition; for example, a painting with a predominant theme of blue might benefit from a touch of a brighter colour such as orange or yellow.

Selective palette

Another way to ensure that there are no jarring notes in your picture is by sticking to a selective range of colours and interweaving them throughout the picture. Using a limited number of colours is an excellent way to learn about colour

mixing – you'll be surprised at the wide range of subtle and vibrant hues that can be mixed from just half a dozen colours.

Try to work over the whole painting at once, so that paint is picked up on the brush and transferred from one area of the composition to another; when a few colours are continually repeated and intermixed in this way, a certain harmony will naturally arise.

Toned grounds

Toning the canvas with a wash of colour is another way of achieving harmony. It is easier to work out a cool colour scheme of blues and greens on a similarly cool blue-grey ground, for example, than on a white ground. The toning strikes through the patches of overlaid paint and becomes an integral part of the picture, pulling together all the various elements.

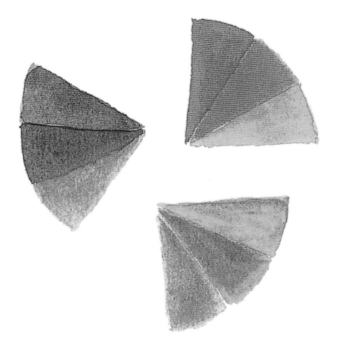

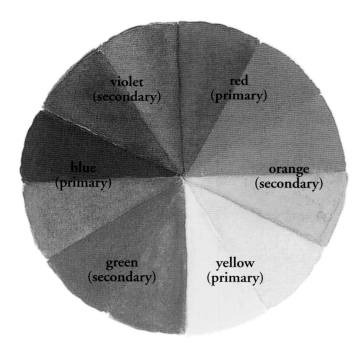

Colours adjacent to one another on the colour wheel form a related, harmonious sequence.

The colour wheel is a handy 'tool' which the artist can refer to when experimenting with colours and the way they react together. It is a simplified version of the spectrum, formed into a circle, showing the arrangement of the primary colours (red, yellow and blue) and the secondary colours (orange, green and violet), from which all other colours are mixed.

79

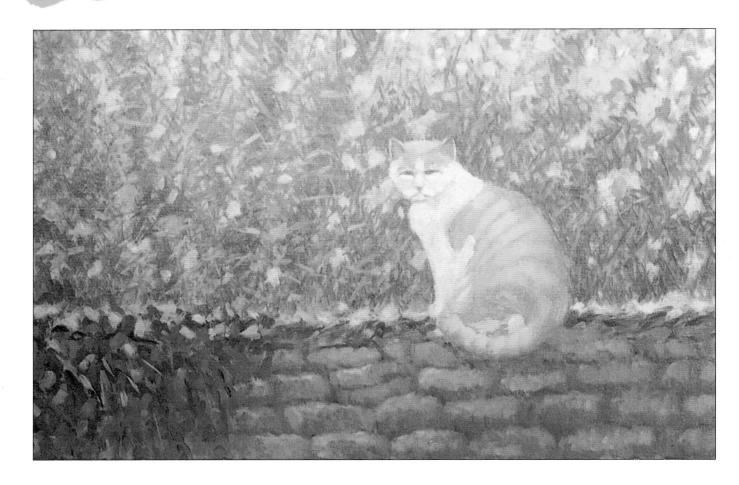

Marmalade Cat

Although this painting contains a lot of complex detail the artist has kept it under control by sticking to a limited palette of related colours. Yellows and oranges predominate, with touches of green providing a foil for the warmer colours. The yellow toned ground strikes through the overlaid brushstrokes, providing a harmonizing element of its own.

YOU WILL NEED

- Sheet canvas or board, 18 x 14in (45.7 x 35.6cm)
- No. 6 round sable or synthetic brush
- No. 8 round bristle brush
- Refined linseed oil
- Distilled turpentine
- Lint-free cloth
- 1½in (38mm) decorating brush

OIL PAINTS IN THE FOLLOWING COLOURS

- Yellow ochre
- Burnt sienna
- Cadmium red
- Titanium white
- Prussian blue
- Cobalt blue
- Lemon yellow
- Cadmium yellow
- Cerulean

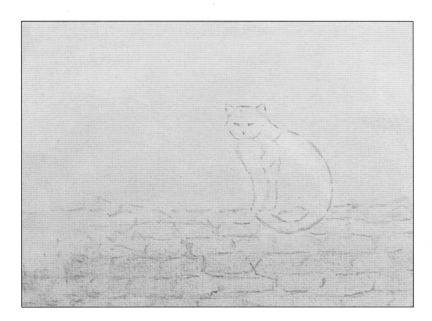

1 Prepare your canvas in advance by toning it with a wash of yellow ochre, well diluted with turpentine and applied with a 1¹/₂in (38mm) decorating brush. Before this dries, rub over the canvas with a clean, lint-free cloth to lighten the colour and soften the brush marks. Leave to dry overnight. This creates a warm, golden undertone that will show through the overlaid colours and harmonize the picture. Sketch the main outlines of the cat and the wall. Use burnt sienna thinly diluted with turpentine, applied with a no. 6 round sable or synthetic brush.

Helpful Hint
TO SAVE TIME, WHY NOT TONE THE CANVAS WITH ACRYLIC PAINT? UNLIKE OILS, THIS DRIES IN MINUTES, ALLOWING YOU TO START PAINTING STRAIGHT AWAY. OIL PAINTS CAN BE APPLIED OVER ACRYLICS, BUT ACRYLICS SHOULD NEVER BE APPLIED OVER OILS AS THIS CAUSES THE OIL PAINT TO CRACK.

2 Use the burnt sienna mix to indicate the striped markings on the cat's coat, then block in the shadows on the face and chest with a pale mix of cadmium red and titanium white, thinly diluted with turpentine and linseed oil. Start work on the foliage in the background with a weak mix of Prussian blue and cadmium red, adding white for the lighter tones. Apply the paint with loose, sketchy strokes, leaving plenty of the ground colour visible.

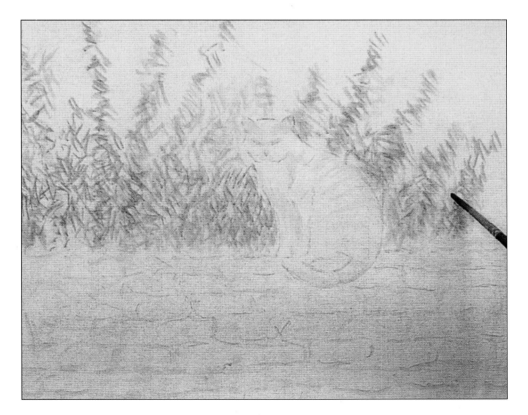

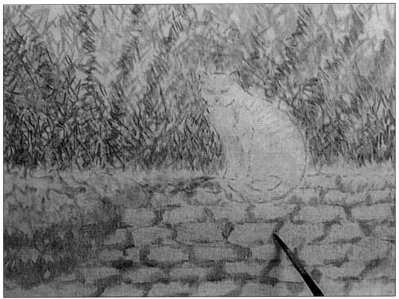

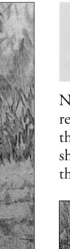

3 Continue working on the foliage, building up the leaves and branches with short, random brushstrokes. Now use the Prussian blue/cadmium red mixture to define the shadows on the individual stones in the wall, and the shadow cast by the ivy climbing over the wall on the left of the picture.

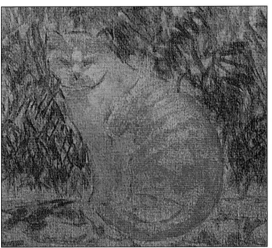

4 Still using the no. 8 brush, mix white with a hint of cobalt blue and carefully paint the pale greyish-white fur on the cat's face and chest with short brushstrokes. Let the pinkish shadows underneath show through the white. Develop the marmalade stripes with a combination of yellow ochre and cadmium red.

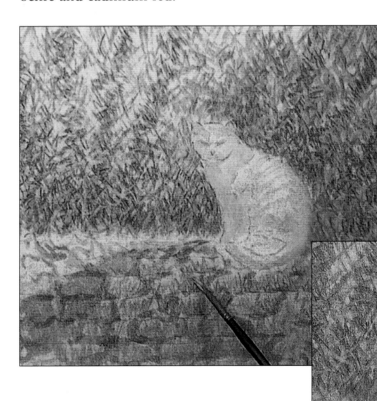

5 Continue working up the background using the same colours as before. Vary the direction of your brushstrokes to suggest the scattered effect of the foliage. Build up the shadows on the wall with loose strokes. The paint should still be quite thin at this stage, allowing the toned ground to show through (see detail). Now make a slightly thicker mix of yellow ochre, cadmium red and white to make a pale peachy colour. Work this loosely into the foliage and on the wall to create soft highlights, flicking the brush gently across the canvas.

6 Mix lemon yellow, cobalt blue and a touch of yellow ochre to make a dull green and start to paint the ivy creeping over the wall. For the light-struck leaves mix together cobalt blue, lemon yellow and white to make a cool blue-green. For the shadows underneath the foliage use a mixture of Prussian blue, cadmium red, yellow ochre and white. Scumble the colour onto the stone wall, still allowing the toned ground to show through.

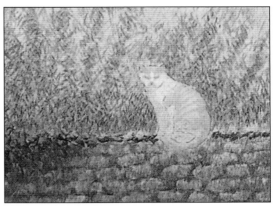

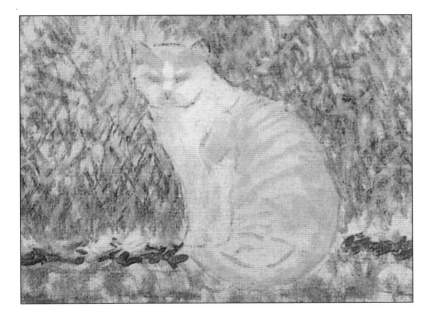

7 Resume work on the cat, adding more of the cobalt blue/white mix for the fur on the face, neck and chest. For the fur between the ears use lemon yellow and white with a touch of cadmium red. Put in the eyes and nose with a dark pink made up of white and cadmium red with a hint of Prussian blue. For the marmalade stripes use white, cadmium yellow, cadmium red and a touch of burnt sienna. Apply the paint with short feathery strokes to give the effect of soft fur.

8 Keep moving from area to area, rather than concentrating on one particular part of the painting. Mix lemon yellow and white and work back into the foliage to introduce some warm highlights with loose dots and dashes. Use the same colour on the ivy along the top of the wall.

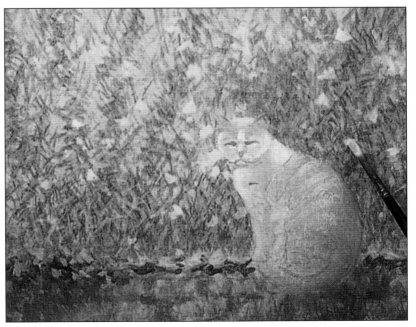

9 Make a thicker mixture of cobalt blue and lemon yellow to make a rich green and use this to build up the foliage, creating a dense patchwork of colour and tone. Then use the white/cobalt blue mix to break a little sky into the foliage at the top of the painting. Switch to a no. 8 round bristle brush and use the same mix to build up the lighter tones on the stone wall.

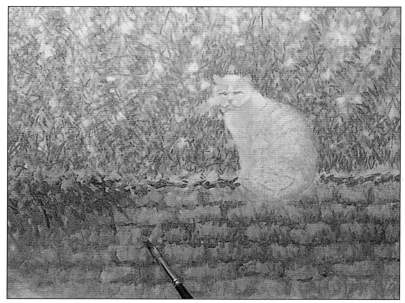

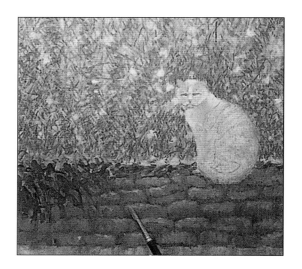

10 Develop the rough texture of the wall with short vertical strokes of thicker paint. Mix cadmium red and Prussian blue to make a dark grey for the shadows between the individual stone slabs, then add a little yellow ochre and white to the mixture to soften the tones. It's important not to let the wall dominate the painting too much – the focus should be on the cat and not on the background.

11 Work over the fur on the cat's face with cadmium yellow to introduce highlights. Paint the ears with a mix of cadmium red, burnt sienna and white, then outline them with a fine line of pure white to separate the cat from the background. Emphasize the striped markings with short strokes of cadmium yellow mixed with white. Add a little cadmium red and yellow ochre to the mixture and darken the orange fur on the back and tail with loose, scumbled strokes.

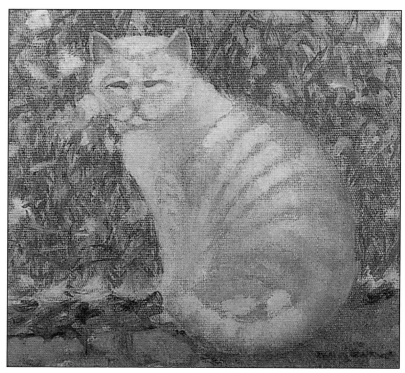

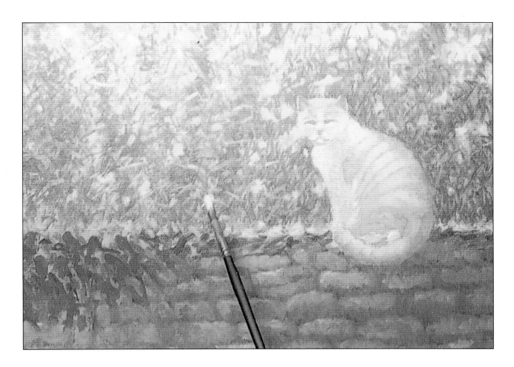

12 Use mixes of cadmium red and Prussian blue to add the deeper tones in the background foliage, then redefine the patches of sky with cobalt blue and white. Moving back to the cat, scumble some strokes of pure white over the fur on the neck and chest to give it a softer appearance. Put in the eyes with a mixture of cadmium red and Prussian blue. Build up the mottled pattern on the stone wall with broken strokes, using varied mixes of yellow ochre, white and touches of cobalt blue.

Helpful Hint
AT AROUND THIS POINT IT'S A GOOD IDEA
TO ALLOW THE PAINT TO DRY FOR 24 HOURS
OR SO BEFORE CONTINUING. IT IS DIFFICULT
TO APPLY THE FINISHING DETAILS ON
TOP OF A WET PAINT SURFACE.

13 To finish the picture, add warmer highlights on the wall with mixes of cerulean, cadmium red and white. Accentuate the highlights on the ivy as well, using cerulean, lemon yellow and white. Repeat some of this colour in the background foliage to provide colour balance. Finally, mix cadmium red and white and suggest some pinkish twigs in the background of the picture with random strokes.

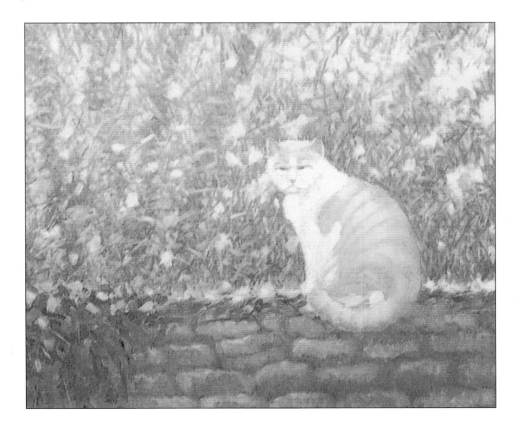

Painting Skies

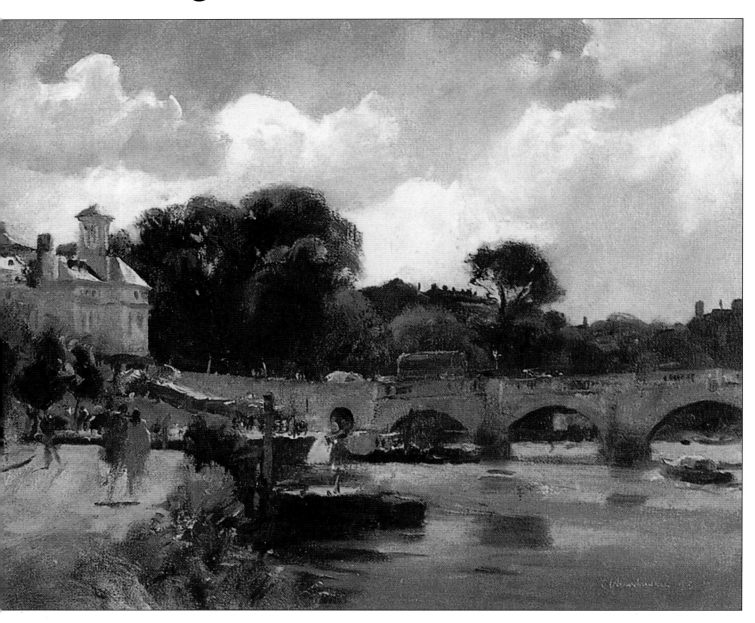

Trevor Chamberlain
SUMMER BY THE RIVER
Clouds directly in front of the sun are exciting to paint because the backlighting makes them appear luminous and gives them a 'silver lining'.

The sky tends to set the mood of a landscape because it is the source of light. It is important, therefore to treat the sky as an integral part of the landscape and not merely as a backdrop. As you paint, try to bring the sky and the land along simultaneously, working from one to the other and bringing some of the sky colour into the land and vice versa.

Techniques

In order to suggest the airiness of the sky and clouds, it is best to work quickly and simplify what you see. Look for the main shapes and block them in with thin paint, then start to introduce detail and modelling. By varying your brushwork and the consistency of the paint, you can create a range of subtle effects that suggest the amorphous nature of clouds and sky. Creamy, opaque colour will suggest groups of dense, advancing clouds; thinly applied, transparent colour gives the impression of atmosphere and receding space, and is ideal for portraying distant clouds and areas of dark, remote sky.

To achieve the effect of distant haze, try blending wet colour into wet, taking some of the sky colour into the land and vice versa. You will find that this slight softening of the horizon gives a marvellous sense of air and light.

Modelling clouds

Look carefully at cloud structure. Clouds are not flat shapes but have three-dimensional form, with distinct planes of light and shadow. Warm colours – reds, oranges and yellows – appear to come forward, as our eyes are more receptive to them. Cool colours – blues, greens and violets – appear to recede. Therefore the contrast of warm and cool colours can be used to model the advancing and receding planes of clouds. The lit areas of cumulus cloud, for example, may contain subtle hints of warm yellow and pink, depending on the weather and the time of day. Those parts of the cloud which are in shadow may appear grey or even brown in colour, and contain blues and violets.

Too many hard outlines make clouds appear 'pasted on' to the sky and destroy the illusion of form. Partially blend the shadow edges of clouds into the surrounding sky so they blend naturally into the surrounding atmosphere.

John Denahy
COASTAL SKY
Instead of painting the sky as a flat area of blue, the artist has used broken strokes of vibrant blues, violets, greens and yellows, laid over a warm-toned ground. This gives a more vivid impression of the sparkle of a summer sky.

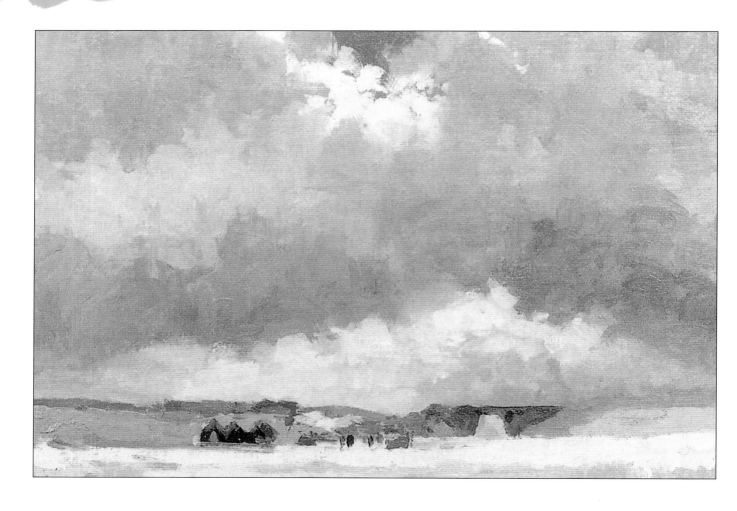

Summer Sky

The sky need not be a mere backdrop to your landscape paintings – it can sometimes be a subject in its own right. In this painting the dramatic clouds form virtually the whole composition, with the narrow strip of hills and fields serving as an anchor to the movement above.

YOU WILL NEED

- [ ] *Sheet of primed board, 12 x 10in (30.5 x 25.4cm)*
- [ ] *No. 3 round sable brush*
- [ ] *No. 4 flat bristle brush*
- [ ] *No. 5 round bristle brush*
- [ ] *Painting knife*
- [ ] *Refined linseed oil*
- [ ] *Distilled turpentine*

OIL PAINTS IN THE FOLLOWING COLOURS

- *Burnt sienna*
- *French ultramarine*
- *Lemon yellow*
- *Ivory black*
- *Titanium white*
- *Alizarin crimson*
- *Cadmium yellow*
- *Cadmium orange*
- *Raw umber*
- *Cerulean*

1 Working on a board tinted with a thin wash of burnt sienna, use a no. 3 round sable brush and diluted burnt sienna to sketch in the details on the horizon. Start by establishing the broad tones in the sky and land using a no. 4 flat bristle brush. For the green fields, mix varying amounts of lemon yellow, French ultramarine, ivory black and titanium white. Rough in the sky using ultramarine, white and a touch of alizarin crimson, plus greys mixed from varied proportions of ultramarine, lemon yellow, black and white.

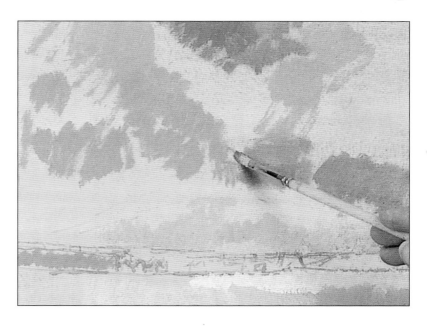

Helpful Hint
LEAVE PATCHES OF THE GROUND BARE IN THE EARLY STAGES SO THAT LATER ADDITIONS OF COLOUR CAN BE SLIPPED INTO THE GAPS. THIS AVOIDS THE DANGER OF OVERWORKING THE AREA WITH PAINT.

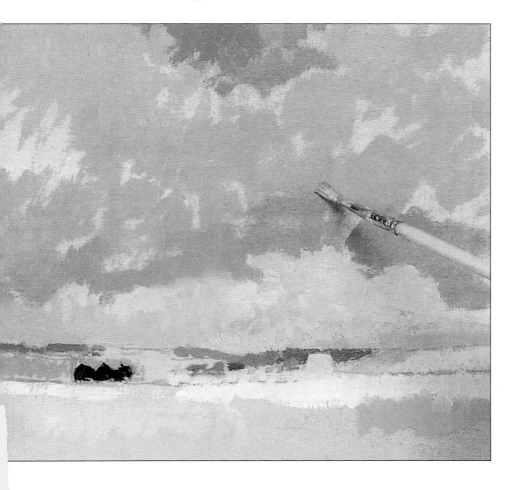

2 Suggest the landscape features in the distance using some of the colours already on your palette. Continue building up the tones in the sky using the same colours mixed in step 1. By varying the proportions of colour used, it is possible to create a wide range of colourful greys ranging from greenish grey through to grey-violet.

3 Work over all the areas of the painting at the same time, moving from the sky to the land and back again and constantly making adjustments to the relative tones and colours. Use a no. 5 round bristle brush to lay in the smaller clouds with rapid brushstrokes, letting some of the colours blend wet-into-wet at the edges.

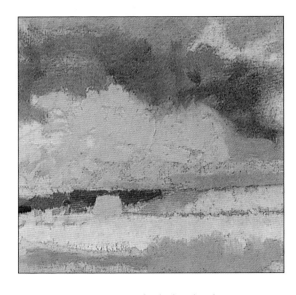

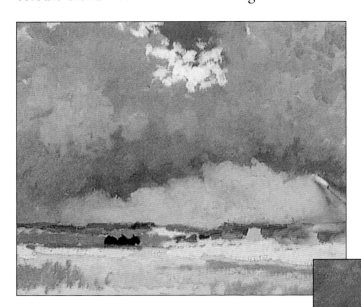

Helpful Hint
TAKE THE TIME TO OBSERVE THE VARIOUS CLOUD TYPES AND THEIR CHARACTERISTICS AND MAKE SKETCHES OF THEM. THESE SKETCHES WILL HELP YOU PAINT SKIES MORE CONVINCINGLY.

4 Begin to use slightly thicker, creamier paint now, and build up the cloud masses with broad strokes, slurring the colours wet-into-wet. Paint the sunlit white cloud with loose strokes of white, warmed with touches of cadmium orange and cadmium yellow. Now work on the large, light cloud on the horizon with a combination of ultramarine, alizarin, raw umber and plenty of white.

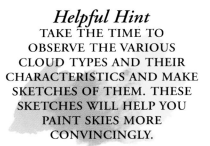

5 Mix a pale, cool grey from ultramarine, alizarin crimson and white and scumble this lightly over the brownish clouds near the top of the sky to give the effect of smaller clouds passing across the large mass of cumulus. Now begin to soften some of the edges of the clouds by blending very gently with a painting knife.

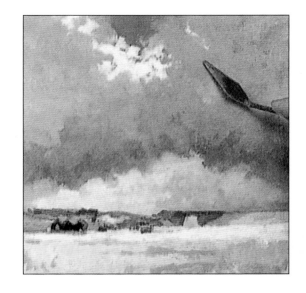

6 At this point it is often a good idea to take a short break from your painting so that you can return to it with a fresh eye and make any necessary corrections or modifications. Here, for example, the cloud mass on the left is a little too heavy, so mix cerulean and white and scumble over the dark grey area to lighten it. Then lighten the brownish area just above it with white, burnt sienna and lemon yellow.

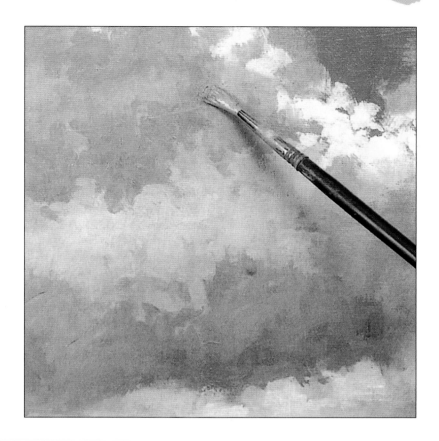

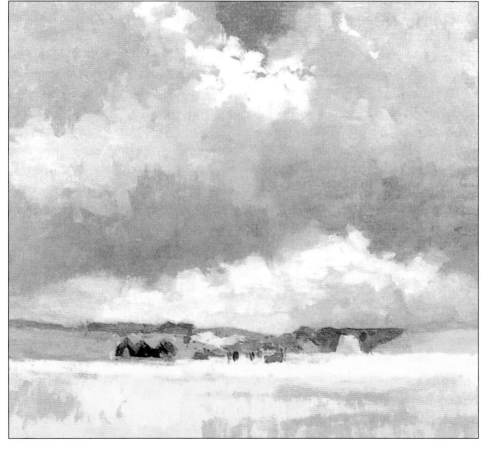

7 Work over the whole picture, modifying colours and softening edges where required; for example, soften the patch of white cloud at the top of the picture to integrate it into the patch of blue sky.

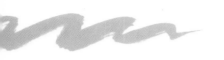

Glossary

Additive A substance such as gum arabic added to paint to alter drying time and viscosity.

Alla prima A term used to describe a work (traditionally an oil painting) that is completed in a single session. Alla prima means "at the first" in Italian.

Colour Complementary: colours that lie opposite one another on the colour wheel.
Primary: The three primary colours cannot be made by mixing other colours. The colours are red, yellow and blue.
Secondary: a colour produced by mixing equal amounts of two primary colours.
Tertiary: a colour produced by mixing equal amounts of a primary colour and the secondary colour next to it on the colour wheel.

Composition The way in which the elements of a drawing are arranged within the picture space.

Drybrush The technique of dragging an almost dry brush, loaded with very little paint, across the surface of the paper to make textured marks.

Fat over lean A fundamental principle of oil painting. In order to minimize the risk of cracking, oil paints containing a lot of oil ('fat' paints) should never be applied over those that contain less oil ('lean' paints) – although the total oil content of any paint mixture should never exceed 50 per cent.

Format The shape of a painting. The most usual formats are landscape (a painting that is wider than it is tall) and portrait (a painting that is taller than it is wide), but panoramic (long and thin) and square formats are also common.

Ground The prepared surface on which an artist works. *See also* Support.

Highlight The point on an object where light strikes a reflective surface.

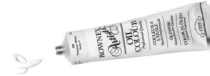

Hue A colour in its pure state, unadulterated by any other colour.

Impasto Impasto techniques involve applying and building oil or acrylic paint into a thick layer. Impasto work retains the mark of any brush or implement used to apply it.

Mahl stick A piece of equipment used in oil painting, consisting of a light rod of wood with a soft leather ball secured on one end.

Mask Any substance that is applied to paper to prevent paint from reaching specific areas. Unlike resists, masks can be removed when no longer required. Masking tape, fluid and film (frisket paper) are used for masking.

Medium
1. The material in which an artist chooses to work pencil, pen and ink, charcoal, soft pastel and so on. (The plural is 'media'.)
2. In painting, 'medium' is also a substance added to paint to alter the way it behaves – to make it thinner, for example. (The plural is 'mediums'.)

Palette
1. The container or surface on which paint colours are mixed.
2. The range of colours used by an artist.

Perspective A system whereby artists can create the illusion of three-dimensional space on the two-dimensional surface of the paper.
Aerial perspective: the way the atmosphere, combined with distance, influences the appearance of things. Also known as atmospheric perspective.

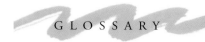

Linear perspective: this exploits the fact that objects appear to be smaller the further away they are from the viewer.

Primer A substance that acts as a barrier between the support and the paint, protecting the support from the corrosive agents present in the paint and the solvents. The traditional primer for use with oil paint is glue size, which is then covered with an oil-based primer such as lead white. Nowadays, acrylic emulsions (often called acrylic gesso) are more commonly used.

Resist A substance that prevents one medium from touching the paper beneath it.

Scaling up A method of transferring an image to a larger format. First, a grid of squares is superimposed on the original image. Then a second grid of larger squares in the same proportion is marked out on the new, larger support. Finally, each square of the original is copied on to the corresponding square on the larger format.

Scumble A technique that involves applying dry, semi-opaque paint loosely and roughly over a dry underlayer, leaving some of the underlayer visible to create optical colour mixes on the support. The technique also produces interesting surface textures.

Sgraffito The technique of scratching off paint to reveal either an underlying paint colour or the white of the paper. The word comes from the Italian verb *graffiare*, which means "to scratch".

Shade A colour that has been darkened by the addition of black or a little of its complementary colour.

Size A weak solution of glue used to make canvas impervious prior to applying layers of primer or oil paint.

Solvent See Thinner.

Spattering The technique of flicking paint on to the paper to create texture.

Sponging The technique of applying colour to the paper with a sponge, rather than with a brush.

Stippling The technique of applying dots of colour to the paper, using just the tip of the brush.

Support The surface on which a painting is made. See also Ground.

Thinner A liquid such as turpentine which is used to dilute oil paint. Also known as Solvent.

Tint A colour that has been lightened.

Tone The relative lightness or darkness of a colour. Also known as Value.

Tonking An technique which involves placing a sheet of newspaper over the wet oil or acrylic paint, smoothing it down and peeling it away to remove excess paint.

Underdrawing A preliminary sketch on the canvas or paper, over which a picture is painted.

Underpainting A painting made to work out the composition and tonal structure of a work before applying colour.

Wash A thin layer of transparent paint that usually covers a large area of the painting.
Flat wash: an even wash with no variation in tone.
Gradated wash: a wash that gradually changes in intensity from dark to light or (less commonly) v.v.
Variegated wash: a wash that changes from one paint colour to another.

Wet into wet Applying paint on to wet paper or on top of an earlier wash that is still damp.

Wet on dry
Applying paint to dry paper or on top of an earlier wash that has dried.

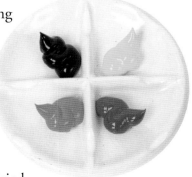

Suppliers

MANUFACTURERS

If you are unable to find what you want in your local art shop, the leading manufacturers of paints, papers and brushes should be able to supply you with details of stockists in your area.

Daler-Rowney UK Ltd
PO Box 10, Bracknell
Berkshire RG12 8ST
United Kingdom
Tel: (01344) 424621
Website: www.daler-rowney.com

Winsor & Newton
Whitefriars Avenue
Wealdston, Harrow
Middlesex HA3 5RH
United Kingdom
Tel: (020) 8427 4343
Website: www.winsornewton.com

H. Schmincke & Co.
Otto-Hahn-Strasse 2
D-40699 Erkrath
Germany
Tel: (0211) 2509-0
Fax: (0211) 2509-461
Website: www.schmincke.de

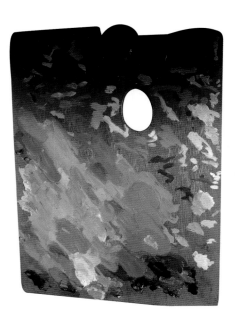

STOCKISTS
United Kingdom

ABS Brushes
Wetley Abbey
Wetley Rocks
Staffordshire ST9 0AS
Tel: (01782) 551551
Email: abs.brushes@btinternet.com
Website: www.absbrushes.com

Art Express
Freepost NEA8739
Leeds LS1 1YY
Freephone: (0800) 731 4185
Website: www.artexpress.co.uk
(Postal address for overseas customers:
Index House, 70 Burley Road,
Leeds LS3 1JX, UK)

Atlantis Art Materials
7–9 Plumbers Row, London E1 1EQ
Tel: (020) 7377 8855
Website: www.atlantisart.co.uk

Dodgson Fine Arts Ltd
t/a Studio Arts
50 North Road
Lancaster LA1 1LT
Tel : (01524) 68014
Email: enquiries@studioarts.co.uk
Website: www.studioarts.co.uk
or www.studioartshop.com

Falkiner Fine Papers
76 Southampton Row
London
WC1B 4AR
Tel: (020) 7831 1151
Email: falkiner@ic24.net

Hobbycraft
Hobbycraft specialize in arts and crafts materials and own 19 stores around the UK. For details of stores near you, phone freephone (0800) 027 2387 or check out the yellow pages or the company's website.
Website: www.hobbycraft.co.uk

Jacksons Art Supplies
PO Box 29568
London N1 4WT
Tel: (0870) 241 1849
Email: sales@jacksonart.com
Website: www.jacksonart.com

Paintworks
99–101 Kingsland Road
London E2 8AG
Tel: (020) 7729 7451
E-mail: shop@paintworks.biz

Russell & Chapel
Tel: (020) 7836 7521

SAA Home Shopping
PO Box 50
Newark
Notts NG23 5GY
Freephone: (0800) 980 1123
Email: homeshopping@saa.co.uk
Website: www.saa.co.uk

Stuart Stevenson
68 Clerkenwell Road
London EC1M 5QA
Tel: (020) 7253 1693

Turnham Arts & Crafts
2 Bedford Park Corner
Turnham Green Terrace
London W4 1LS
Tel: (020) 8995 2872

United States
Many of these companies operate retail outlets across the US. For details of stores in your area, check out the yellow pages or the relevant website.

Art & Frame of Sarasota
1055 South Tamiami Trail
Sarasota FL 34236
Tel: (941) 366-2301
Toll Free: (800) 393-4278
Email: orders@in2art.com
Website: www.in2art.com

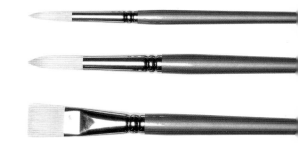

Dick Blick Art Materials
PO Box 1267
Galesburg, IL 61402-1267
Tel: (800) 828-4548
Website: www.dickblick.com
(More than 30 stores in 12 states.)

Hobby Lobby
Website: www.hobbylobby.com
(More than 300 stores in 27 states.)

Michaels Stores
Michaels.com
8000 Bent Branch Dr.
Irving TX 75063
Tel: (1-800) 642-4235
Website: www.michaels.com
(More than 750 stores in 48 states.)

Mister Art
913 Willard Street
Houston TX 77006
Tel (toll-free): (866) 672-7811
Website: www.misterart.com.

The Easel Studio
Tel (toll-free): (800) 916-2278
E-mail: bobbielarue@yahoo.com
Website: www.easelstudio.com

Canada
Artists in Canada
803 Brightsand Terrace
Saskatoon, Saskatchewan, S7J 4X9
Website: www.artistsincanada.com

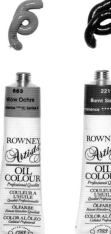

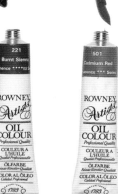

D. L. Stevenson & Son Ltd
1420 Warden Avenue
Scarborough, Ontario M1R 5A3.
Tel: (416) 755-7795
E-mail (Canada):
colourco@interlog.com
E-mail (US): customer service@
artpaintonline.com

Buy customized paper and canvas
stretchers from:
Upper Canada Stretchers Inc.
1750 16th Avenue East
Box 565 Owen Sound
Ontario, N4K 5R4
Tel: (1-800) 561-4944
Email: donato@ucsart.com
Website: www.ucsart.com

The Paint Spot
Tel: (800) 363 0546
Website: www.paintspot.ca

Colours Artist Supplies
414 Graham Avenue
Winnipeg, Manitoba R3C 0L8
Tel: (204) 956-5364,
Email: colours@mb.sympatico.ca
(6 stores across western Canada)

Australia
Art Materials
Website: www.artmaterials.com.au

Dick Blick Art Materials
Customer Service: (800) 723-2787
Product Info: (800) 933-2542
International: (309) 343-6181
E-mail: info@dickblick.com
Website: www.dickblick.com

Madison Art Shop
Tel: (800) 961-1570
Website: www.MadisonArtShop.com

MasterGraphics Inc.
810 West Badger Road
Madison WI 53713
Tel: (608) 256-4884
Toll Free: (800) 873-7238
E-mail: mastergraphics@masterg.com
Website: www.masterg.com

North Shore Art Supplies
10 George Street
Hornsby, New South Wales
Tel: (02) 9476 0202

Oxford Art Supplies Pty Ltd
CITY
221–223 Oxford Street
Darlinghurst
NSW 2010
Tel: (02) 9360 4066
Email: orders@oxfordart.com.au
Website: www.oxfordart.com.au
or www.janetsart.com.au

Oxford Art Supplies and Books
Pty Ltd
Chatswood
145 Victoria Ave
Chatswood
NSW 2067.
Tel: (02) 9417 8572

New Zealand
Draw Art Supplies Ltd.
PO Box 24022
5 Mahunga Drive
Mangere Bridge
Auckland
Tel: (09) 636 4989
E-mail: enq@draw-art.co.nz
Website: www.draw-art.co.nz

Fine Art Supplies
PO Box 58 018,
38 Neil Park Dr.
Greenmount
Auckland
New Zealand
Tel: (64-9) 274 8896
Website: www.fineart supplies.co.nz

Index

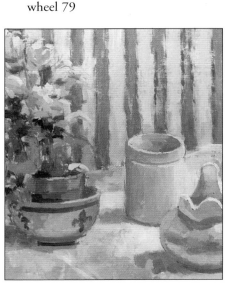